Teens
at Risk

OPPOSING
VIEWPOINTS®

OTHER BOOKS OF RELATED INTEREST

OPPOSING VIEWPOINTS SERIES

America's Children
Child Abuse
Child Welfare
Crime and Criminals
Gangs
Juvenile Crime
Media Violence
Suicide
Teenage Pregnancy
Teenage Sexuality
Tobacco and Smoking
Violence

CONTEMPORARY ISSUES COMPANION SERIES

Eating Disorders

CURRENT CONTROVERSIES SERIES

Crime
Family Violence
Smoking
Teen Addiction
Violence in the Media
Youth Violence

AT ISSUE SERIES

Date Rape
Rape on Campus
Sex Education
Single-Parent Families
Smoking

Teens
at Risk

OPPOSING
VIEWPOINTS®

WITHDRAWN

David L. Bender, *Publisher*
Bruno Leone, *Executive Editor*
Bonnie Szumski, *Editorial Director*
Brenda Stalcup, *Managing Editor*
Scott Barbour, *Senior Editor*
Laura K. Egendorf, *Book Editor*
Jennifer A. Hurley, *Book Editor*

OPPOSING
VIEWPOINTS®
SERIES

Greenhaven Press, Inc., San Diego, California

Library of Congress Cataloging-in-Publication Data

Teens at risk : opposing viewpoints / Laura K. Egendorf, book editor,
Jennifer A. Hurley, book editor.
    p.   cm. — (Opposing viewpoints series)
    Includes bibliographical references and index.
    ISBN 1-56510-949-X (lib. bdg. : alk. paper). —
ISBN 1-56510-948-1 (pbk. : alk. paper)
    1. Socially handicapped teenagers—United States. 2. Problem
youth—United States. 3. Juvenile delinquency—United States.
4. Teenage pregnancy—United States. 5. Teenagers—Substance
use—United States. I. Egendorf, Laura K., 1973– . II. Hurley,
Jennifer A., 1973– . III. Series.
HV1431.T44 1999
362.74—dc21

                                 98-23191
                                      CIP

Greenhaven Press, Inc., P.O. Box 289009
San Diego, CA 92198-9009

"CONGRESS SHALL MAKE NO LAW...ABRIDGING THE FREEDOM OF SPEECH, OR OF THE PRESS."

First Amendment to the U.S. Constitution

The basic foundation of our democracy is the First Amendment guarantee of freedom of expression. The Opposing Viewpoints Series is dedicated to the concept of this basic freedom and the idea that it is more important to practice it than to enshrine it.

CONTENTS

Chapter 3: How Can Teen Pregnancy Be Prevented?

Chapter 4: What Role Do the Media and Government Play in the Problem of Teen Substance Abuse?

WHY CONSIDER OPPOSING VIEWPOINTS?

"The only way in which a human being can make some approach to knowing the whole of a subject is by hearing what can be said about it by persons of every variety of opinion and studying all modes in which it can be looked at by every character of mind. No wise man ever acquired his wisdom in any mode but this."

John Stuart Mill

In our media-intensive culture it is not difficult to find differing opinions. Thousands of newspapers and magazines and dozens of radio and television talk shows resound with differing points of view. The difficulty lies in deciding which opinion to agree with and which "experts" seem the most credible. The more inundated we become with differing opinions and claims, the more essential it is to hone critical reading and thinking skills to evaluate these ideas. Opposing Viewpoints books address this problem directly by presenting stimulating debates that can be used to enhance and teach these skills. The varied opinions contained in each book examine many different aspects of a single issue. While examining these conveniently edited opposing views, readers can develop critical thinking skills such as the ability to compare and contrast authors' credibility, facts, argumentation styles, use of persuasive techniques, and other stylistic tools. In short, the Opposing Viewpoints Series is an ideal way to attain the higher-level thinking and reading skills so essential in a culture of diverse and contradictory opinions.

In addition to providing a tool for critical thinking, Opposing Viewpoints books challenge readers to question their own strongly held opinions and assumptions. Most people form their opinions on the basis of upbringing, peer pressure, and personal, cultural, or professional bias. By reading carefully balanced opposing views, readers must directly confront new ideas as well as the opinions of those with whom they disagree. This is not to simplistically argue that everyone who reads opposing views will—or should—change his or her opinion. Instead, the series enhances readers' understanding of their own views by encouraging confrontation with opposing ideas. Careful examination of others' views can lead to the readers' understanding of the logical inconsistencies in their own opinions, perspective on why they hold an opinion, and the consideration of the possibility that their opinion requires further evaluation.

EVALUATING OTHER OPINIONS

To ensure that this type of examination occurs, Opposing Viewpoints books present all types of opinions. Prominent spokespeople on different sides of each issue as well as well-known professionals from many disciplines challenge the reader. An additional goal of the series is to provide a forum for other, less known, or even unpopular viewpoints. The opinion of an ordinary person who has had to make the decision to cut off life support from a terminally ill relative, for example, may be just as valuable and provide just as much insight as a medical ethicist's professional opinion. The editors have two additional purposes in including these less known views. One, the editors encourage readers to respect others' opinions—even when not enhanced by professional credibility. It is only by reading or listening to and objectively evaluating others' ideas that one can determine whether they are worthy of consideration. Two, the inclusion of such viewpoints encourages the important critical thinking skill of objectively evaluating an author's credentials and bias. This evaluation will illuminate an author's reasons for taking a particular stance on an issue and will aid in readers' evaluation of the author's ideas.

As series editors of the Opposing Viewpoints Series, it is our hope that these books will give readers a deeper understanding of the issues debated and an appreciation of the complexity of even seemingly simple issues when good and honest people disagree. This awareness is particularly important in a democratic society such as ours in which people enter into public debate to determine the common good. Those with whom one disagrees should not be regarded as enemies but rather as people whose views deserve careful examination and may shed light on one's own.

Thomas Jefferson once said that "difference of opinion leads to inquiry, and inquiry to truth." Jefferson, a broadly educated man, argued that "if a nation expects to be ignorant and free . . . it expects what never was and never will be." As individuals and as a nation, it is imperative that we consider the opinions of others and examine them with skill and discernment. The Opposing Viewpoints Series is intended to help readers achieve this goal.

David L. Bender & Bruno Leone,
Series Editors

Greenhaven Press anthologies primarily consist of previously published material taken from a variety of sources, including periodicals, books, scholarly journals, newspapers, government documents, and position papers from private and public organizations. These original sources are often edited for length and to ensure their accessibility for a young adult audience. The anthology editors also change the original titles of these works in order to clearly present the main thesis of each viewpoint and to explicitly indicate the opinion presented in the viewpoint. These alterations are made in consideration of both the reading and comprehension levels of a young adult audience. Every effort is made to ensure that Greenhaven Press accurately reflects the original intent of the authors included in this anthology.

INTRODUCTION

"Suicide is the nation's second leading cause of death among teenagers."

—Chintan Turakhia

"For both sexes and all races, teenagers experience the lowest suicide rates of any age group except pre-teens."

—Mike Males

According to a 1997 nationwide survey conducted by the Public Agenda Foundation and the Advertising Council, a vast majority of adults—nine out of ten—are pessimistic about the future of today's youth. As analysts of the survey conclude, "Americans are convinced that today's adolescents face a crisis." Many social critics contend that the stresses of modern-day society—including violence in the schools, deteriorating family security, and an overdose of disturbing media images—put teens at risk of never reaching their full potential. Teens who have trouble coping with such enormous pressures, some maintain, resort to drug and alcohol use, violence, sexual relationships that often result in pregnancy or sexually transmitted diseases, and sometimes suicide.

However, other commentators criticize the tendency to view teenagers as "troubled" and insist that today's teenagers face no more hardships than those of past generations. Furthermore, these critics argue that many of the problems teens encounter—in particular, academic competition, financial worries, and relationship issues—are nothing new. As writer Andrea Young Ward contends, "Gangs and drug abuse are not unique to the '90s." In fact, some say that the elimination of social taboos, which previously prevented people from speaking openly about sex, drugs, and other sensitive issues, has made it easier for teenagers to cope with problems.

In judging the condition of today's youth, researchers often look to suicide rates as an indicator of how teens are doing. Some assert that teen suicide rates are rising, reflecting an overall downward trend for today's youth. The American Association of Suicidology reports that between 1980 and 1994, suicide rates increased 30 percent for teens aged fifteen to nineteen. The increase in teenage suicide rates, observers claim, is glaring evidence that teens are distressed, desperate, and without hope for the future.

These commentators allege that among certain groups of teenagers, the incidence of suicide is rising at a horrifying rate. For example, according to one statistic, the suicide rate for fifteen- to nineteen-year-old black males has increased 164 percent between 1980 and 1992—and continues to rise. Moreover, many researchers believe that a significant number of suicides committed by young African-American males go unreported. As columnist Fern Shen notes, the suicide of adolescent black males "often is masked by labels such as 'drug overdose' or by situations in which the victim purposely provokes a police officer or other person to kill him." Journalist and political commentator Clarence Page refers to the tendency of young black males to place themselves in highly dangerous situations as "suicide by other means."

Another group at a high risk of suicide, some maintain, is gay teens. According to a 1989 report by the Department of Health and Human Services, 30 percent of five hundred gay and lesbian youths interviewed in San Francisco had attempted suicide at least once. Social critics say that the isolation gay teens experience, due to fears of rejection or attempts to conceal their sexual identity, puts them at a serious risk of suicide. Furthermore, notes one government study, gay teens are more likely to engage in the types of behaviors that increase their chances of committing suicide, including drug use and sexual activity.

With surveys documenting that 60 percent of teens personally know a teenager who has tried to commit suicide, it seems as though suicide is pandemic among today's youth. However, the notion that teen suicide rates are skyrocketing does not go undisputed. A number of critics maintain that flawed statistics create a deceptive picture about teens. Mike Males, author of *The Scapegoat Generation: America's War on Adolescents*, offers a different explanation for the increasing numbers of teen suicides. In the past, he maintains, many teen suicides committed with a firearm were labeled "accidents" due to the social stigma surrounding teenage suicide; today, the correct labeling of firearm deaths as suicides gives the false impression that teen suicide has increased, when actually it has remained nearly the same.

Moreover, some argue that teen suicide rates do not provide a clear picture of the condition of teens in general. For example, according to Males, teen suicide rates in the state of California have decreased by 30 percent since 1970, despite the concurrent rise in homelessness, AIDS, and gang violence—not to mention a greater availability of guns and deadly drugs. The fact that teen suicide is declining while risky behavior is increasing, claim observers, suggests that teen suicide might not be an accurate way to assess the overall situation of teens.

Furthermore, says Males and others, teenage suicide, while horrible from any standpoint, can be put into perspective when the rate of teen suicide is compared to that of other age groups. Excluding young children, teenagers are the least likely group to commit suicide—far less likely than adults. In fact, the group most likely to commit suicide is the elderly, who have a suicide rate 2.5 times that of teenagers.

Numerous researchers also dispute the notion that gay teenagers are at a high risk of committing suicide. While a variety of media sources have reported that gay and lesbian teenagers are two to three times more likely than heterosexual teens to commit suicide, other commentators contend that these claims are unsubstantiated. They allege that the statistic about gay teen suicides originated from a single essay written by a San Francisco social worker who based his figures on methodologically flawed studies. In fact, a 1994 panel composed of social analysts and mental health advocates found that "there is no population-based evidence that sexual orientation and suicidology are linked in some direct or indirect manner."

Some of those who feel teen suicide is not as common as it is portrayed to be argue that it is dangerous to overstate the problem of teen suicide: If teens feel "everybody is doing it," they may begin to view suicide as an acceptable way of coping with their struggles. Others declare that "copycat suicides" are a myth. As Mary Kluesner, President of Suicide Awareness/Voices of Education notes, "There are no documented scientific studies, only rumor and assumed belief, that contagion is a reality. Suicide contagion is very, very rare."

The suicide rate is just one barometer of the quality of teens' lives. Other signals include the rates of teen pregnancy, drug use, and crime. These and other issues are addressed in *Teens at Risk: Opposing Viewpoints*, which contains the following chapters: What Factors Put Teens at Risk? How Can Society Deal with Teenage Crime and Violence? How Can Teen Pregnancy Be Prevented? What Role Do the Media and Government Play in the Problem of Teen Substance Abuse? Throughout these chapters, the authors assess the risks that today's teens face and present potential solutions to these problems.

WHAT FACTORS PUT TEENS AT RISK?

CHAPTER PREFACE

Former vice president Dan Quayle brought the issue of single parenthood into the limelight in the early 1990s, when he criticized the television show *Murphy Brown* for its positive portrayal of single parenthood. Quayle and a number of other commentators argue that teenagers from single-parent families are more inclined to engage in risky behavior than those from traditional two-parent families. David Popenoe, a critic of single parenthood, maintains that "the decline of fatherhood is a major force behind . . . crime and delinquency; premature sexuality and out-of-wedlock births to teenagers; deteriorating educational achievement; [and] depression, substance abuse, and alienation among adolescents."

Those who allege that single parenthood puts teenagers at risk cite two reasons for their views. First, they claim, children in single-parent families receive half of the attention, supervision, and financial resources as those from two-parent families. Second, critics of single-parent families maintain, children without fathers miss out on critical lessons about competition, initiative, risk-taking, and independence.

However, others dismiss the notion that a traditional family structure is essential to raising a child successfully. They contend that other familial factors, not single parenthood, influence teen behavior. For example, the National Longitudinal Study on Adolescent Health found that the most important deterrent to risky adolescent behavior was "a feeling of connectedness and love from parents"—a conclusion that held true for both single- and two-parent families. David Demo, a professor at the University of Carolina, argues that because of idyllic television families such as the Cunninghams of the program *Happy Days* and the Cleavers of *Leave It to Beaver*, "a lot of people just assume that [the two-parent family] is the healthiest, ideal family structure." When it comes to the well-being of teenagers, however, Demo maintains that "family structure is not the most important influence."

Those who believe single-parent families place teenagers at risk feel that the only solution is a return to the traditional family structure. Those who view single parenthood as a viable alternative to two-parent families say that society should focus on helping single parents succeed, rather than criticizing them. The question of whether single parenthood puts teens at risk, along with related issues, is debated in the following chapter.

> "Up to 15% of 16- to 19-year-olds are at risk of never reaching their potential and simply becoming lost in society."

A VARIETY OF FACTORS PUT TEENS AT RISK

Gene Stephens

Gene Stephens contends in the following viewpoint that a variety of factors are responsible for the risks teens face. He maintains that today's teens are at risk due to a combination of social problems—including teenage pregnancy, the growing number of single-parent families, poverty, and child abuse—as well as individual problems such as truancy, substance abuse, and feelings of hopelessness. In order to help teens at risk, Stephens advocates the implementation of community-based youth programs. Stephens is a professor of criminal justice at the University of South Carolina.

As you read, consider the following questions:
1. How does Stephens define "at risk" teens?
2. In the author's opinion, how does teen pregnancy place youths at risk?
3. What are the eight characteristics of Stephens's plan to help teens at risk?

Reprinted from Gene Stephens, "Youth at Risk: Saving the World's Most Precious Resource." This article originally appeared in the March/April 1997 issue of The Futurist. Used with permission from the World Future Society, 7910 Woodmont Ave., Suite 450, Bethesda, MD 20814.

Child-care advocates claim that up to 15% of 16- to 19-year-olds are at risk of never reaching their potential and simply becoming lost in society. Others would add to this category children of any age if they are at risk of not becoming self-supporting adults, headed for a life in institutions for delinquency, crime, mental illness, addiction, and dependency. We could also describe as "at risk" those teens and preteens who take on child rearing themselves and drop out of school.

The task of saving these children has become increasingly formidable. Compounding the problem are the expanding gap between the rich and poor, the increasing number of single-parent households, the rise of homes where both parents work, the growing gun culture, and the recent increase in negative attitudes about children, such as courts that treat younger and younger children as adult criminals.

As a result, children lose hope for the future. They turn to peers for attention; they turn to guns for protection, security and status; and they turn to sex and drugs for comfort and relief of boredom. The gang too often becomes their "family"—the only place where they receive attention and approval.

Criminologist James Fox of Northeastern University predicts that the murders committed by teenagers (4,000 in the United States in 1995) will skyrocket as the 39 million children now under age 10 swell the ranks of teenagers by 20% in the first decade of the twenty-first century. The result could be a juvenile crime wave such as the United States has never seen.

SIGNS OF HOPE

Yet, such a catastrophe is not inevitable. There are some signs of hope: a slightly decreased birth rate among teenagers in the mid-1990s, a rising bipartisan concern about "saving the children," burgeoning community-based experiments for meeting the needs of youth, and a movement to regard poor prenatal care, poor parenting skills, child abuse, and child neglect as public-health problems.

Beyond this, a striking change in the rearing of children in many families has been observed. Countering the trend toward ignoring or even abusing children is a trend toward cherishing and nurturing them. Thousands or even millions of young parents are taking turns working while the other stays at home and makes child care almost a full-time vocation. There is an unrecognized renaissance in parenting progressing quickly in neighborhoods across the nation and possibly the world.

Of course, having youth at risk is not a problem unique to

the United States. Wars, social upheaval, rapidly changing economic systems, political instability, and cultural animosity have placed millions of children at risk around the world. Children die of starvation while others wander aimlessly in search of home and family.

Juvenile Arrests, 1980 to 1994

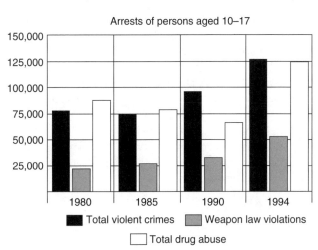

Arrests of persons aged 10–17

■ Total violent crimes ▨ Weapon law violations ☐ Total drug abuse

U.S. Federal Bureau of Investigation, *Statistical Abstract of the United States* 1996.

Singling out specific problems is difficult, for most are interrelated. For example, children left alone without adult attention are more likely to experiment with sex and drugs. Teenagers who try drugs are more likely to be involved in delinquent behavior. Children who experiment with sex increase their likelihood of becoming unmarried teenage parents. Youngsters who are physically and sexually abused are more likely to adopt abusive behavior toward others. Clearly, however, the following are major factors in the dilemma.

Teenage Pregnancy
Many child advocates see teenage pregnancy as the main problem. Children having children puts both generations at risk and often leads to poverty, poor health care, truancy, and underemployment. The dimensions of the issue—as reported by the National Commission on Children, the United States Census Bureau, and others—are staggering:
  • Every year, one in 10 teenage females becomes pregnant—

more than 3,000 a day.

- One of four teenage mothers will have a second child within one year of her first child's birth.
- Most teenage mothers are single and receive no support from the father.
- Eight of 10 teenage mothers do not finish high school.

THE ROLE OF SINGLE PARENTHOOD

About one-fourth of the families in America are headed by a single parent—usually the mother. In the Hispanic community, it is one-third; among black families, it is one-half. Most of the children in these families were born to teenagers.

According to the Centers for Disease Control (CDC), 85% of all children exhibiting behavioral disorders come from father-less homes. Other statistical findings indicate that children from fatherless homes are: 32 times more likely to run away; nine times more likely to drop out of high school; 14 times more likely to commit rape; 10 times more likely to be substance abusers; and 20 times more likely to end up in prison.

POVERTY AND POOR HEALTH CARE

Whereas 75% of single-female-headed households are in poverty at least some of the time, and 33% are chronically poor, poverty is also endemic to a majority of young households. Already, one in three children under 6 lives below the poverty line.

About half of the homeless are families with children. A million divorces each year create new female-headed households below the poverty line.

CDC and other agencies have found that at least 25 million children in the United States have no health care. This means that they are taken to the hospital emergency room or to non-professionals for health problems. Without change in health provider arrangements, half of the nation's children could be without health care by the year 2000. Already, most unwed mothers receive no prenatal care.

Lack of health care too often equals stunted ability to learn, life-altering health problems, lowered ability to cope in a free-market system, and, as a result, greater likelihood of drug abuse, delinquency, and crime.

CHILD ABUSE

There is substantial evidence of child abuse or neglect in the background of every known serial killer. In most cases, the abuse was physically or sexually severe.

Beyond blatant abuse, neglect itself—ignoring the child's physical and emotional needs—is a form of abuse that scars the child as much or more than beatings.

Child abuse and neglect are often called the "silent epidemic" in the United States. Alleged abuse more than quadrupled between the mid-1970s and the mid-1990s to more than 3 million cases a year reported (and 1 million substantiated). A Gallup Poll reported that physical abuse cases were 16 times greater than reported rates, and sexual abuse was 10 times greater.

The U.S. Department of Justice reports that abused or neglected children are 40% more likely to be arrested as juvenile delinquents and adult criminals; three times as likely to use drugs and alcohol, get into fights, and deliberately damage property; and four times as likely to steal and be arrested. It is also reported that one in eight neglected children was later arrested for a violent offense.

CHRONIC TRUANCY AND SCHOOL DROPOUT

On the average school day, as many as 15% of junior and senior high school students are not in school. For too many, this is a pattern that leads to dropout.

Truants represent a large portion of those arrested for daytime break-ins and thefts, and dropouts are over-represented in jails and prisons.

The Census Bureau reports that earnings of students without a high school diploma average far below the poverty line.

ALCOHOL AND DRUG ABUSE

Polls of youth indicate that nine out of 10 teenagers drink alcohol to some extent by the time they finish high school, and a majority have used illegal drugs. A study of 1,200 school dropouts in California found their weekly alcohol-use rates were twice as high as in-school counterparts, and their use of hard drugs was two to five times as high. Dropout drug users were much more likely to be involved in violent and criminal activities. One-third said they had sold drugs in the past year, and twice as many dropouts as in-school students said they belonged to a gang.

The Gallup Poll reported that 70% of 16- to 24-year-olds believe that the world was a better place when their parents were their age, and 56% said it will be worse for their own children. A joint *Washington Post*, Kaiser, and Harvard survey reported that the belief that "most people can be trusted" fell from 54% to 35%, and trust in government dropped from 76% to 25% over a three-decade period ending in 1995. At-risk youth, in particular, say they "live for today" and see no hope for their future.

CRIME AND HOMICIDE

In 1996, the Justice Department reported that the juvenile homicide rate had almost doubled in over a decade, and blacks and males were by far the most likely to be killed.

The major correlating factor was an increase in the use of firearms. Guns were also found to be the single factor that could account for tripling the number of juvenile homicide offenders over the decade. Justice predicts another doubling of crime by juveniles by 2010 if current trends continue.

Tragically, most victims of juvenile violence are other juveniles, often children who are not even involved in the dispute. . . .

A PLAN TO HELP TEENS AT RISK

The plan that follows represents a consensus from groups to whom I've given the same assignment over the past decade: "Develop a program to turn your community's youth into productive, happy, law-abiding adults." These groups have included students from high school to graduate school, practitioners from police to social service workers, and community leaders, all participating in brainstorming and planning sessions to alleviate the youth-at-risk problem.

Here is a comprehensive plan based on my 10-plus years' experience with these exercises.

1. Commit to positive reinforcement through community and school-based parenting classes (mandatory in schools), ongoing media campaigns, positive attention, and recognition in all schools (preschool through high school) and community-based programs.

2. Promote nonviolent conflict resolution among peers through mandatory educational programs for students, parents, teachers, counselors, administrators, media, and community campaigns.

3. Encourage mentoring for all children. Civic, business, and community campaigns should recruit and train mentors, matching them by needs and temperament. Programs such as Big Brothers and Big Sisters should be expanded.

4. Establish community-school partnerships to offer before- and after-school tutoring. Enlist youth to perform services to the community to enhance their stake in society.

5. Develop community-oriented proactive policing programs that begin with a philosophy of prevention. Examples of prevention programs include midnight basketball leagues, police-youth athletic leagues, neighborhood housing project substations, and foot pa-

trols. These all involve partnerships of police, parents, church, business, civic, and community organizations.

6. *Initiate ethical and cultural awareness programs* that build on partnerships among family, church, school, media, civic, business, and other community groups. These programs would emphasize finding common ground on basic values, such as respect, responsibility, and restraint.

7. *Design youth opportunity programs* to provide all children the chance to reach their potential, regardless of circumstances. Such programs could be run through school, business, and community partnerships that provide in-school jobs and child care, career counseling and training, opportunity scholarships, and recognition for achievement.

8. *Set up peer counseling hotlines* to help youth help each other through the trying times of adolescence.

To this basic plan we may also consider in the future adding more dramatic (though often controversial) measures, such as birth-control implants, health monitoring and treatment implants, behavioral control implants in extreme cases, computer-assisted brain implants, and educational implants. But these measures should only be considered after reaching consensus concerning ethical issues.

In addition, we must focus on justice where delinquency and crime occur. Youth offenders must recognize the consequences of their actions on the victim, the victim's family, and the community. The harm must be ameliorated and restored through mediation and arbitration, restitution, service to the victim and community, reclamation, and reconciliation.

CHILDREN WANT ATTENTION

Every community can develop programs guided by this model. But all plans must adopt certain guiding principles that permeate the approach.

Children want attention above everything. Thus, giving attention reinforces behavior and denying attention extinguishes behavior. Both praise and punishment are attention, and both will reinforce behavior that gets that attention.

It is important to instill optimism and faith in the future in all children, as they are the key to success. The very nature of adolescence is to challenge authority, but most children drift through this troubled period and become law-abiding adults unless they become labeled as delinquents, criminals, or losers.

Surely we can see the need to reach out and lend a hand to the world's most precious resource.

> "U.S. teenagers today are, by nearly every important measure, healthier, better educated, and more responsible than teens of the past."

TEENS ARE NOT AT RISK

Kirk A. Astroth

In the following viewpoint, Kirk A. Astroth refutes the notion that today's teens are at risk; in fact, Astroth claims, statistics show that older generations are generally worse off than teenagers. He maintains that the portrayal of teens as troubled and "out of control" is solely a product of ephebiphobia—adults' fear and hatred of adolescents. Astroth is an extension specialist in the State 4-H Office at Montana State University, Bozeman.

As you read, consider the following questions:

1. According to Astroth, what is responsible for the rise in teen admissions to psychiatric hospitals?
2. In the author's view, why are the statistics on teen suicide misleading?
3. What groups are more likely to commit suicide than teens, in Astroth's opinion?

Reprinted from Kirk A. Astroth, "Beyond Ephebiphobia: Problem Adults or Problem Youths?" *Phi Delta Kappan*, January 1994, by permission of the author and Phi Delta Kappa International.

It is common today to hear that almost half of all young people between the ages of 10 and 17 are at risk of school failure, substance abuse, delinquency, and teenage pregnancy. Indeed, it would appear that troubled youths are no longer the exception but have become the dysfunctional rule. Young people today are typically portrayed as an aberrant pariah class that suffers its own distinct "epidemics" bearing no relationship to adult patterns of behavior. Are today's young people really so different?

Given the barrage of adolescent problems uncovered by so-called researchers, it should come as a shocking surprise to learn that U.S. teenagers today are, by nearly every important measure, healthier, better educated, and more responsible than teens of the past. Moreover, the Iowa Youth Poll for 1991, published by the Iowa State University Extension Service, revealed that most young people feel satisfied with their lives and generally positive about themselves.

Today's Teens Lead Healthy Lives

Not only are today's teens healthier than teens of the past, but they are typically healthier than the adults who seem so ready to label them as "at risk." Even in such cities as Los Angeles, it is estimated that 90% to 95% of all young people are not involved in gangs. Yet we are bombarded with alarms about rising gang activity in our big cities.

Like previous generations of adults, we appear to be suffering from ephebiphobia—a fear and loathing of adolescence. Nearly every generation of young people has been chastised for being "out of control" or aberrant in some way. Adult claims of degeneration among the young can be found in nearly every previous decade. For example, the cover of the 6 September 1954 issue of Newsweek blared: "Let's Face It: Our Teen-Agers Are Out of Control." The article inside lamented a "national teen-age problem—a problem that is apparently getting worse." And why? "Too much divorce, too few normal homes," claimed one sociologist. Others denounced "salacious, sadistic comic books." Today, we might blame MTV.

Adults Are Biased Against Teens

Unfortunately, the notion of "youth at risk" has become a lens through which we view all young people, so that today adolescence is seen as some incurable social disease. For example, a study of teenage drinking in the 1950s describes patterns that are the same as those of teens today. In reality, today's teens behave in ways very similar to those of teens of the past and very much like those of today's adults.

The recent sharp increase in teen psychiatric admissions is one manifestation of our pathological treatment of today's youth. Since 1980 adolescent psychiatric admissions have increased 250% to 400%, but "it's not because teens are suddenly so much crazier than they were a decade ago," according to Lynette Lamb. The Children's Defense Fund suggests that at least 40% of these juvenile admissions are inappropriate, may violate the civil rights of the "patients," and are a result of parents' inability to deal with adolescent behavior.

TEENS ARE MUCH LESS LIKELY THAN ADULTS TO COMMIT SUICIDE

U.S. suicides per 100,000 persons of each age group, sex, and race, 1991

Age group	Total	Male	Female	White	Nonwhite
10–14	1.5	2.3	0.7	1.6	1.0
15–19	11.0	17.6	3.7	11.8	7.8
All 10–19	6.2	10.0	2.2	6.7	4.4
20–24	14.9	25.4	3.9	13.6	11.3
25–34	15.2	25.0	5.4	16.0	11.3
35–44	14.7	24.0	6.5	15.9	8.1
All 20–44	14.9	24.7	5.5	15.5	9.9
45–64	15.5	24.4	7.1	16.6	7.9
Over 65	19.7	40.2	6.0	21.0	8.4
All ages >10	14.4	23.9	5.6	15.5	8.4

National Center for Health Statistics, *Vital Statistics of the United States 1991*, 1995.

Though commonplace, such a pathological perspective on adolescence exaggerates the negative. Stanton Peele, a Princeton University psychologist, has observed that today's views often define adolescence itself as a diseased state. He points out that research is usually skewed toward the maladjusted young, which has created a myth of the prevalence of adolescent maladjustment.

As astonishing as it may sound, today's teens lead healthier lives than most young and middle-aged adults. Teens have lower rates of suicide, violent death, unwed pregnancy, drug abuse, smoking, and drunken driving. When youth problems do occur, adult influence is apparent. For example, in Montana "nearly 60% of 'teen' pregnancies are [caused] by men over the age of 21," according to Mike Males. Only 29% of all "teen" pregnancies actually involve two teenagers. The most important thing adults can do about the "epidemic of teen pregnancy" in Montana and other states is to stop impregnating teenagers.

AN "EPIDEMIC" OF TEEN SUICIDE?

To illustrate the point that we've become too negative about the current generation of young people, let's look at one other area: teen suicide. The oft-quoted statistics cited to dramatize this epidemic are that nearly 6,000 teens kill themselves annually and that suicides have tripled since the 1950s. But let's look at the data.

First, we have to ask ourselves what seems like a simple question: Who is a teenager? Federal data for 1990 show 13.6 suicides per 100,000 population for people between the ages of 15 and 24. The "teen" suicide rate of 6,000 comes from this same age group—a group that includes more than just teens. What we also fail to ask is how this rate compares to the rate for other age groups. If we are going to be accurate when we discuss "teen" suicide, we should be looking at the suicide rate for 13- to 19-year-olds, not 15- to 24-year-olds. Census data show that the suicide rate for 10- to 19-year-olds is about 10 per 100,000, one of the lowest rates for any age group. More teens die each year from cancer (13 per 100,000) than from suicide.

While I don't wish to minimize the tragedy of any pointless deaths, especially teen suicides, I want us to put the issue in perspective and stop needlessly alarming communities about a "teen suicide epidemic." If we are truly concerned about high suicide rates, we should be devoting more attention to older citizens. Senior citizens over the age of 85 have a suicide rate of 22.5 per 100,000—2.5 times the rate for 10- to 19-year-olds. Those between 75 and 84 years of age have a suicide rate of 26.1 per 100,000; those between 65 and 74 years of age have a suicide rate of 18.1 per 100,000. And rates for Americans 65 and older rose 21% from 1980 to 1986. So who's at risk?

In 1956, 10,000 teens died from violent causes, including 1,100 from firearms (a toll that almost surely includes many hidden suicides) and 5,200 from traffic deaths. This total death rate has changed little over the years. What has changed, though, is our honesty about how teens die. During the 1950s, many deaths from firearms were classified as "accidental"; we now accurately list them as suicides.

ADULTS COMMIT SUICIDE MORE THAN TEENS

The reality is that teens as a whole are less likely to commit suicide than any other age group except preteens. In fact, Montana's teen suicide rate is not rising, and youth suicide levels and trends appear to be linked to those of adult suicide. Occupational surveys consistently show that parents and teachers are twice as likely, counselors and psychologists are four times as likely, and school administrators are six times as likely to commit suicide as are high school students. Today's teens are more justified in worrying that a parent, adult relative, teacher, or counselor will commit suicide than the other way around. Yet we do not question the health of all grown-ups as a result.

Today's mythology that most or all youths are "at risk" scatters valuable resources and dilutes efforts to help the minority of youths who are genuinely troubled. While the problems faced by our young people are serious, I want to caution against framing the issue as an "epidemic." Certainly, some of our young people are troubled. Precisely because such problems as suicide, drug addiction, and delinquency are enormous tragedies, we must be clear about the nature and extent of the problems as we study and seek to prevent them. Blanket approaches that inflate the numbers of youths "at risk" are not only ineffective but also undermine the effectiveness of what should be carefully targeted preventive measures.

> "If I were a Hollywood producer who put before the eyes of impressionable kids images that glorify violence . . . , I would find it awfully hard to sleep at night."

MEDIA VIOLENCE PUTS TEENS AT RISK

Mona Charen

In the following viewpoint, Mona Charen maintains that violent media images inspire teens to commit violent crimes. Because children are saturated in violent media from such an early age, the author claims, they become numb to violence and are therefore prone to aggressive behavior. Charen is a syndicated columnist.

As you read, consider the following questions:

1. On what basis does Charen state that the nation suffers from a "moral meltdown"?
2. What inspired fourteen-year-old Michael Carneal to open fire on a group of friends, according to Charen?
3. In the author's opinion, how is the entertainment media able to influence actions?

Reprinted from Mona Charen, "Do Movies Make Kids Kill?" *Conservative Chronicle*, December 24, 1997, by permission of Mona Charen and Creators Syndicate.

It is sad evidence of our internal carnage that we seem to have become an expert nation of mourners. The latest version, from Paducah, Ky., was so well stage-managed and professional—complete with live coverage by CNN—that it seemed almost planned.

The 14-year-old accused killer, Michael Carneal, entered his high school during the pre-school hours carrying five guns. He found the room where a group of his friends were holding a prayer meeting and began shooting to kill. Three girls were shot dead. Another six were wounded. One is permanently paralyzed from the waist down.

The young man in custody is described by one and all as the product of a good family. His father is a prominent Paducah attorney. The family attends church regularly. The accused killer's sister will be valedictorian this year at the high school now stained with blood. The boy himself, while small and unprepossessing, was at no time considered to be unbalanced or mentally disturbed.

He was, by all accounts, a fairly normal boy who seethed at being the butt of teasing by his contemporaries, leaving the troubling question: How could a normal child commit such a despicable crime? How could he shoot down his friends in cold blood?

A MORAL MELTDOWN

The overall crime rate in the United States is dropping. And while this is reassuring news, it does not quiet the concern that this nation is in the grip of a serious moral meltdown. For while the absolute number of crimes is down, the nature of crimes committed, particularly by the very young, continues to shock and dismay us.

Normal teenaged girls have given birth in toilet bowls and then left their offspring in trash bins. Other normal kids have lured strangers to their homes—in New Jersey it was a pizza delivery man—for the pure pleasure of killing. In New York in 1997, two middle-class teenagers killed a wino they had met in Central Park and then attempted to mutilate his body so that police would be unable to identify him.

The streets of inner cities are pockmarked by the sites of casual murders; murders for sneakers, murders for clothes, murders over basketball games and murders because someone "dissed" someone else.

Michael Carneal says he was inspired by the movie *The Basketball Diaries*, which features a dream sequence in which a kid who is teased gets revenge by killing his classmates with a shotgun. The scenes are vivid and gory. At first blush, they would seem to repel anyone.

Horsey. Reprinted by special permission of North America Syndicate.

But our kids are marinated in violence from an early age. The images they see and hear—from Nine Inch Nails to Marilyn Manson—are so grotesque that they dull the senses.

Now it is fashionable to say that Hollywood never made anyone pick up a gun, that the people who do kill would have done so anyway and copycat crimes merely reflect the lack of creativity on the part of criminals.

HOW THE MEDIA ENCOURAGES VIOLENCE

Nonsense. The entertainment media convey a sense of what is within the realm of the possible. If everyone on prime-time television is sleeping around, there is no question that this influences the viewers' sense of what is proper and acceptable. A few years ago, the movie *The Money Train* portrayed a criminal firebombing the ticket booth of a New York subway. Within a few weeks of the movie's release, three copycat crimes had taken place. Harry Kaufman, who worked inside one of those booths, was condemned to days of torture from third-degree burns and ultimately death.

The veneer of civilization is very thin. Almost all of us have

31

the capacity under the right circumstances to behave savagely. Some of us need only a little encouragement.

Clearly, the causes of violence are complex. But there have always been tormented teenagers. Only recently have they thought it reasonable to blow their classmates away with shotguns. If I were a Hollywood producer who put before the eyes of impressionable kids images that glorify violence and revel in pornography (the sexual and the violent kind), I would find it awfully hard to sleep at night.

| "Claims that TV causes violence bear
| little relation to real behavior."

MEDIA VIOLENCE DOES NOT PUT TEENS AT RISK

Mike Males

Mike Males, author of *The Scapegoat Generation: America's War on Adolescents*, argues in the following viewpoint that real violence, not media violence, is responsible for juvenile crime. He maintains that teens who engage in risky behavior are often mimicking the behavior of their parents or other adults, not the violence they see depicted in television programs, films, and other media.

As you read, consider the following questions:

1. What proof does Males offer that media violence does not cause teen violence?
2. According to Males, what is America's "biggest explosion in felony violence"?
3. In the author's opinion, what influence do cigarette ads have on teens?

Reprinted from Mike Males, "Stop Blaming Kids and TV," *The Progressive*, October 1997, by permission of *The Progressive*, 409 E. Main St., Madison, WI 53703.

"Children have never been very good at listening to their elders," James Baldwin wrote in *Nobody Knows My Name*. "But they have never failed to imitate them." This basic truth has all but disappeared as the public increasingly treats teenagers as a robot-like population under sway of an exploitative media. White House officials lecture film, music, Internet, fashion, and pop-culture moguls and accuse them of programming kids to smoke, drink, shoot up, have sex, and kill.

So do conservatives, led by William Bennett and Dan Quayle. Professional organizations are also into media-bashing. In its famous report on youth risks, the Carnegie Corporation devoted a full chapter to media influences.

Progressives are no exception. *Mother Jones* claims it has "proof that TV makes kids violent." And the Institute for Alternative Media emphasizes, "the average American child will witness . . . 200,000 acts of [TV] violence" by the time that child graduates from high school.

THE PREVALENCE OF REAL VIOLENCE

None of these varied interests note that during the eighteen years between a child's birth and graduation from high school, there will be fifteen million cases of real violence in American homes grave enough to require hospital emergency treatment. These assaults will cause ten million serious injuries and 40,000 deaths to children. In October 1996, the Department of Health and Human Services reported 565,000 serious injuries that abusive parents inflicted on children and youths in 1993. The number is up four-fold since 1986.

The Department of Health report disappeared from the news in one day. It elicited virtually no comment from the White House, Republicans, or law-enforcement officials. Nor from Carnegie scholars, whose 150-page study, "Great Transitions: Preparing Adolescents for a New Century," devotes two sentences to household violence. The left press took no particular interest in the story, either.

All sides seem to agree that fictional violence, sex on the screen, Joe Camel, beer-drinking frogs, or naked bodies on the Internet pose a bigger threat to children than do actual beatings, rape, or parental addictions. This, in turn, upholds the Clinton doctrine that youth behavior is the problem, and curbing young people's rights the answer.

Claims that TV causes violence bear little relation to real behavior. Japanese and European kids behold media as graphically brutal as that which appears on American screens, but seventeen-year-olds in those countries commit murder at rates lower than those of American seventy-year-olds.

Likewise, youths in different parts of the United States are exposed to the same media but display drastically different violence levels. TV violence does not account for the fact that the murder rate among black teens in Washington, D.C., is twenty-five times higher than that of white teens living a few Metro stops away. It doesn't explain why, nationally, murder doubled among nonwhite and Latino youth over the last decade, but declined among white Anglo teens. Furthermore, contrary to the TV brainwashing theory, Anglo sixteen-year-olds have lower violent-crime rates than black sixty-year-olds, and Anglo thirty-year-olds. Men, women, whites, Latinos, blacks, Asians, teens, young adults, middle-agers, and senior citizens in Fresno County—California's poorest urban area—display murder and violent-crime rates double those of their counterparts in Ventura County, the state's richest.

Confounding every theory, America's biggest explosion in felony violent crime is not street crime among minorities or teens of any color, but domestic violence among aging, mostly white baby boomers. Should we arm Junior with a V-chip to protect him from Mom and Dad? . . .

CHILDREN IMITATE ADULTS

I worked for a dozen years in youth programs in Montana and California. When problems arose, they usually crossed generations. I saw violent kids with dads or uncles in jail for assault. I saw middle-schoolers molested in childhood by mom's boyfriend. I saw budding teen alcoholics hoisting forty-ouncers alongside forty-year-old sots. I also saw again and again how kids start to smoke. In countless trailers and small apartments dense with blue haze, children roamed the rugs as grownups puffed. Mom and seventh-grade daughter swapped Dorals while bemoaning the evils of men. A junior-high basketball center slept outside before a big game because a dozen elders—from her non-inhaling sixteen-year-old brother to her grandma—were all chain smokers. Two years later, she'd given up and joined the party.

As a rule, teen smoking mimicked adult smoking by gender, race, locale, era, and household. I could discern no pop-culture puppetry. My survey of 400 Los Angeles middle schoolers for a 1994 *Journal of School Health* article found children of smoking parents three times more likely to smoke by age fifteen than children of non-smokers. Parents were the most influential but not the only adults kids emulated. Nor did youngsters copy elders slavishly. Youths often picked slightly different habits (like chewing tobacco, or their own brands).

In 1989, the Centers for Disease Control lamented, "75 percent of all teenage smokers come from homes where parents smoke." You don't hear such candor from today's put-politics-first health agencies. Centers for Disease Control tobacco chieftain Michael Eriksen informed me that his agency doesn't make an issue of parental smoking. Nor do anti-smoking groups. Asked Kathy Mulvey, research director of INFACT: "Why make enemies of fifty million adult smokers" when advertising creates the real "appeal of tobacco to youth?"

MEDIA VIOLENCE DOES NOT MAKE TEENS KILL

Thirty-one suburban and rural California counties, with a population of 2.5 million, including 250,000 teenagers, had no teenage murders in 1993. Yet in a state with 4,000 murders that year, these kids saw the same movies, heard the same music, possessed as many guns as those central Los Angeles census tracts with the same youth population, but with more than 200 youth murders. One difference: The youth poverty level of those thirty-one suburban and rural counties is tiny in comparison with central L.A.

Alexander Cockburn, *Nation*, June 3, 1996.

Do ads hook kids on cigarettes? Studies of the effects of the Joe Camel logo show only that a larger fraction of teen smokers than veteran adult smokers choose the Camel brand. When asked, some researchers admit they cannot demonstrate that advertising causes kids to smoke who would not otherwise. And that's the real issue. In fact, surveys found smoking declining among teens (especially the youngest) during Joe's advent from 1985 to 1990.

The University of California's Stanton Glantz, whose exposure of 10,000 tobacco documents enraged the industry, found corporate perfidy far shrewder than camels and cowboys.

"As the tobacco industry knows well," Glantz reported, "kids want to be like adults." An industry marketing document advises: "To reach young smokers, present the cigarette as one of the initiations into adult life . . . the basic symbols of growing up."

The biggest predictor of whether a teen will become a smoker, a drunk, or a druggie is whether or not the child grows up amid adult addicts. Three-fourths of murdered kids are killed by adults. Suicide and murder rates among white teenagers resemble those of white adults, and suicide and murder rates among black teens track those of black adults. And as far as teen pregnancy goes, for minor mothers, four-fifths of the fathers are adults over eighteen, and half are adults over twenty.

The inescapable conclusion is this: If you want to change juvenile behavior, change adult behavior. But instead of focusing on adults, almost everyone points a finger at kids—and at the TV culture that supposedly addicts them.

Groups like Mothers Against Drunk Driving charge, for instance, that Budweiser's frogs entice teens to drink. Yet the 1995 National Household Survey found teen alcohol use declining. "Youths aren't buying the cute and flashy beer images," an in-depth USA Today survey found. Most teens found the ads amusing, but they did not consume Bud as a result.

By squabbling over frogs, political interests can sidestep the impolitic tragedy that adults over the age of twenty-one cause 90 percent of America's 16,000 alcohol-related traffic deaths every year. Clinton and drug-policy chief Barry McCaffrey ignore federal reports that show a skyrocketing toll of booze and drug-related casualties among adults in their thirties and forties—the age group that is parenting most American teens. But both officials get favorable press attention by blaming alcohol ads and heroin chic for corrupting our kids.

Progressive reformers who insist kids are so malleable that beer frogs and Joe Camel and Ace Ventura push them to evil are not so different from those on the Christian right who claim that Our Bodies, Ourselves promotes teen sex and that the group Rage Against the Machine persuades pubescents to roll down Rodeo Drive with a shotgun.

America's increasingly marginalized young deserve better than grownup escapism. Millions of children and teenagers face real destitution, drug abuse, and violence in their homes. Yet these profound menaces continue to lurk in the background, even as the frogs, V-chips, and Mighty Morphins take center stage.

> "Children living in homes where fathers are absent are far more likely to be expelled from or drop out of school, develop emotional or behavioral problems, commit suicide, and fall victim to child abuse or neglect."

THE ABSENCE OF FATHERS PUTS TEENS AT RISK

Wade F. Horn

The number of single-parent families rose from 8 million in 1960 to 24 million in 1995. Wade F. Horn maintains in the following viewpoint that this increase in fatherless families has caused widespread violence, pregnancy, and drug abuse among teenagers. Fathers are an essential part of a child's successful upbringing, the author contends. Horn is a clinical child psychologist, a faculty member at Georgetown University's Public Policy Institute, and president of the National Fatherhood Initiative.

As you read, consider the following questions:

1. According to Horn, what are the two mechanisms by which parents socialize children?
2. In the author's view, why are fathers important?
3. What does Horn cite as the consequences of fatherlessness?

Reprinted from Wade F. Horn, "Why There Is No Substitute for Parents," *Imprimis*, June 1997, by permission of *Imprimis*, the monthly journal of Hillsdale College.

In 1960, the total number of children living in fatherless families was fewer than eight million. Today, that total has risen to nearly twenty-four million. Nearly four out of ten children in America are being raised in homes without their fathers and soon it may be six out of ten. How did this happen? Why are so many of our nation's children growing up without a full-time father? It is because our culture has accepted the idea that fathers are superfluous—in other words, they are not necessary in the "modern" family. Supposedly, their contributions to the well-being of children can easily be performed by the state, which disburses welfare checks, subsidizes midnight basketball leagues, and establishes child-care facilities.

Ideas, of course, have consequences. And the consequences of this idea have been as profound as they have been disastrous. Almost 75 percent of American children living in fatherless households will experience poverty before the age of eleven, compared to only 20 percent of those raised by two parents. Children living in homes where fathers are absent are far more likely to be expelled from or drop out of school, develop emotional or behavioral problems, commit suicide, and fall victim to child abuse or neglect. The males are also far more likely to become violent criminals. As a matter of fact, men who grew up without dads currently represent 70 percent of the prison population serving long-term sentences.

Undeniably, fathers *are* important for the well-being of children. So, too, are traditional families. They ensure the continuity of civilization by propagating the species and socializing children. Everyone seems to understand the obvious benefits of propagation, but the important role that parents play in socializing children is widely misunderstood and undervalued.

WHY SOCIALIZATION IS IMPORTANT

Socialization can be defined as the process whereby individuals acquire the behavior, attitudes, and values that are not only regarded as desirable and appropriate by society but that have also stood the test of time and proved to be the most humane. Proper socialization requires delaying or inhibiting "impulse gratification" in order to abide by the rule of law and the rule of custom. Well-socialized children have learned, for example, not to strike out at others to get what they want; poorly socialized children have not. Well-socialized children have learned to obey the directions of legitimate authority figures like parents and teachers; poorly socialized children have not. Well-socialized children have learned to cooperate and share with others; poorly socialized children have not.

Much of what is described as "good character" or "virtue" reflects the ability to delay or inhibit impulse gratification. When a child tells the truth, even though he knows that it will result in negative consequences, he is inhibiting the impulse to lie to avoid unpleasantness. When he shows charity to others, he is inhibiting the impulse to behave selfishly. A civil society is dependent upon virtuous citizens who have developed this capacity to delay or inhibit impulse gratification; that is, persons who can control their behavior voluntarily. Without a majority of such citizens, storekeepers would have to post armed guards in front of every display counter, women would live in constant fear of being raped by roaming bands of marauding men, and children would be left to the mercy of those who would exploit them. Fortunately, well-socialized children generally become well-socialized adults. Unfortunately, poorly socialized children generally do not. There are few statements one can make with complete certitude, but here is one: When families fail in their task to socialize children, a civil society is not possible. Herein lies the awesome responsibility of parenting.

TWO MECHANISMS OF SOCIALIZATION

Parents socialize children through two mechanisms. The first is teaching through direct instruction reinforced by a combination of rewards and punishments for acceptable and unacceptable behavior. The second is teaching by example. Of the two, the latter is the more important mechanism since most complex human behavior is acquired through observational learning. Children are much more likely to do as a parent *does* than as a parent *says*. This is why parents who lie and cheat tend to raise children who lie and cheat, despite any direct instruction to the contrary. As Benjamin Franklin once observed, the best sermon is indeed a good example.

Please note that I have not asserted that the state—or as it is euphemistically referred to these days, the "village"—is necessary for the proper socialization of children. Rather, it is parents who are necessary, and this means a mother *and* a father. There are, of course, thousands of single mothers who are doing a heroic job of parenting and beating the odds. I do not mean to denigrate their efforts. Yet there is a great deal of hard evidence to suggest that when fathers are absent, boys tend to develop poor conduct. They "act out" their aggressive impulses, sometimes quite violently toward others. Girls also tend to act out when fathers are absent, but in a different way; they become rebellious and promiscuous.

MOTHERS AND FATHERS PARENT DIFFERENTLY

No matter what the advocates of "gender-free parenting" may say, mothers and fathers do parent differently. Mothers tend to be more verbal, whereas fathers are more physical. Mothers also tend to encourage personal safety and caution, whereas fathers are more challenging when it comes to achievement, independence, and risk-taking. And mothers tend to be stronger comforting figures than fathers who are more intent upon establishing and enforcing rules governing the behavior of their children.

The fact that mothers and fathers parent differently is not to say that one group does it "right" or "better" than the other. What children need to develop good character is the combination of what mothers and fathers bring to the parenting equation. Take the fact that mothers tend to be nurturers and fathers tend to be disciplinarians. Parenting experts used to believe that families socialize children best when both parents adopt a nurturing but permissive role, demonstrating high levels of love and low levels of control. Decades of research have shown, however, that when children are reared this way they act out through chronic bad behavior. Permissiveness as a "parenting style" simply doesn't work. Boys and girls need a high level of nurturing balanced by a high level of control. Those who are reared in families that exhibit this combination are friendlier, more energetic, and better behaved. Those who are reared by single mothers, therefore, are warm and affectionate but have difficulty learning self-discipline. Conversely, those who are reared by single fathers are obedient but often plagued by anxiety and insecurity.

WHY ARE FATHERS IMPORTANT?

It has also been fashionable for those pushing for gender-free parenting to assert that the physical play of fathers has no beneficial impact on child-rearing. Many self-proclaimed child experts exhort fathers to stop playing with the kids and do more housework. Some even claim that the rough-and-tumble play of fathers teaches aggression and should be avoided. But new clinical studies reveal that the physical play of fathers actually gives children much-needed practice in regulating their emotions and behavior and helps them develop the capacity to recognize the emotional cues of others.

The point is not to force a choice between the parenting role of mothers or fathers but to suggest that they work best when they work together. This view contrasts sharply with the "two pair of hands" argument, which holds that when it comes to parenting, two people are better than one and it makes no difference whether they are mothers or fathers. In reality it matters greatly to whom the "two pairs of hands" are attached. Kids don't need impersonal "caregivers"; they need loving moms and dads.

Reprinted by permission of Chuck Asay and Creators Syndicate.

Fathers are also critical to the proper socialization of children because they teach by example how to keep negative impulses in check. It is through boys' observation of the way their fathers deal with frustration, anger, and sadness that they learn how men should cope with such emotions. It is also through the observation of how fathers treat mothers that boys learn how men should treat women. If fathers treat mothers with dignity and respect, then it is likely that their sons will grow up to treat women with dignity and respect. If fathers treat mothers with contempt and cruelty, then it is likely that their sons will, too. Fathers are also critical for the healthy emotional development of girls. If girls experience the love, attention, and protection of fathers, then they are likely to resist the temptations of seeking such things elsewhere—often through casual sexual relations at a very young age. Finally, fathers are important in helping children make the difficult transition to the adult world. Boys require an affirmation that they are "man enough." Girls require an affirmation that they are "worthy enough."

Given this understanding, what should we expect when fatherlessness becomes the norm? We don't need a crystal ball to find the answer. As I indicated earlier, nearly four out of every ten children are being raised absent their fathers right now. The result is that juveniles are the fastest growing segment of the criminal population in the United States. Between 1982 and 1991, the rate at which children were arrested for murder increased 93 percent; for aggravated assault, 72 percent; for rape, 24 percent; and for automobile theft, 97 percent. Although homicide rates have increased for all ages, those for teenagers have increased more rapidly than for adults.

The teen population is expected to grow by 20 percent over the next decade, and this is precisely the generation most likely to be reared without fathers. The prospect has led many sociologists, criminologists, and law enforcement agencies to conclude that shortly after the turn of the twenty-first century we will see an adolescent crime wave the likes of which has never been seen before in this country. If that were not enough, we know that each and every day:

- 7,700 children become sexually active;
- 1,100 children have abortions;
- 2,500 children are born out of wedlock;
- 600 children contract syphilis or gonorrhea; and
- six children commit suicide.

Fatherlessness is not solely responsible for these tragedies, but it certainly is a major cause. Indeed, all the available evidence suggests that improving the well-being of our children—and ultimately our nation—depends upon finding ways to bring fathers back into the home.

| "Most children of single parents do not drop out of school, get arrested, abuse drugs, or suffer long-term emotional distress."

THE ABSENCE OF FATHERS DOES NOT PUT TEENS AT SIGNIFICANT RISK

Stephanie Coontz

Stephanie Coontz maintains in the following viewpoint that broad generalizations about the risks associated with single parenthood perpetuate the myth that two-parent families are always better than single-parent families. In fact, she contends, there are potential advantages and disadvantages to both single-parent and two-parent families. Moreover, the author argues that two-parent families that are abusive or conflict-ridden can be more harmful to children than families in which no father is present. Stephanie Coontz, a family historian at the Evergreen State College in Olympia, Washington, wrote *The Way We Never Were: American Families and the Nostalgia Trap* (1992) and *The Way We Really Are: Coming to Terms with America's Changing Families* (1997).

As you read, consider the following questions:

1. According to the author, what are the potential disadvantages of two-parent families?
2. What does Coontz cite as the potential advantages of single-parent families?
3. What are the greatest periods of stress for two-parent families and for single-parent families, in the author's view?

Excerpted from Stephanie Coontz, "The American Family and the Nostalgia Trap," *Phi Delta Kappan*, March 1995, by permission of the author and Phi Delta Kappa International.

There is no denying that children need more than one caring adult in their lives, or that family breakup is a potent cause of childhood distress. Why, then, complain "profamily" advocates, can't we simply revive the "cultural consensus" that, "on the average, an intact, two-parent family is best"?

The problem is that such seemingly innocuous generalizations encourage preconceived notions that a particular "intact" family does have a responsible, involved mother and father and that a particular single-parent or reconstituted family does not have its own strengths. People end up in single-parent homes for a variety of reasons, some of which even the most radical right-wingers would acknowledge as valid. And there is much wider variation among children from single-parent families, including never-married ones, than there is between the averages for each category.

GENERALIZATIONS ABOUT DIVORCED FAMILIES

Broad generalizations about family types ignore critical variations and usually reflect serious methodological errors. For example, in 1989 Judith Wallerstein published a long-term study of middle-class children of divorced families, claiming that almost half of the children of divorced parents experience long-term pain, worry, and insecurity that adversely affect their love and work relationships. It was Wallerstein's work that laid the foundation for Barbara Whitehead's claim in the April 1993 *Atlantic Monthly* that "the evidence is in." But this supposedly definitive study was based on a self-selected sample of only 60 couples. It did not compare the children of divorced couples with those of nondivorced ones to determine whether some of their worries and adjustment problems might have stemmed from other factors, such as work pressures, general social insecurities, or community fragmentation. Moreover, the sample was drawn from families already experiencing difficulty and referred to a divorce clinic for therapy. According to Andrew Cherlin and Frank Furstenberg, "Only a third of the sample was deemed to possess 'adequate psychological functioning' prior to the divorce."

More careful research yields much lower estimates of the risks associated with single parenthood. In February 1993 Paul Amato published a review of nearly every single quantitative study that had been done on divorce. Although he found some clear associations with lower levels of children's well-being, these were, on average, "not large." A meta-analysis of such studies, published in the *Psychological Bulletin*, also found "modest" differences overall, noting that the more carefully controlled the studies, the smaller the differences they reported. The "large majority" of children of divorce, wrote 11 family researchers in response to Whitehead's misuse of their data, do not experience long-term problems. Most children of single parents do not drop out of school, get arrested, abuse drugs, or suffer long-term emotional distress. Only a minority of such children do experience severe problems. Meanwhile, children from high-conflict marriages or even ones in which the father has simply withdrawn often do worse in the long run than do children of divorced or never-married parents. A RAND Corporation study reports that marital conflict has a stronger relation with youthful delinquency and aggression than does parental absence per se. . . .

STIGMATIZATION HARMS SINGLE-PARENT FAMILIES

Certainly, one-parent families face serious challenges. After all, it's hard enough for two parents to raise children in a society in which rampant consumerism is constantly rubbing against rampant inequality. But most families can meet the challenges, so long as these are not multiplied by intense economic stress, deteriorating social support systems, and the very same social stigma that the family-values crusaders believe to be part of the cure for our family problems. Indeed, one review of the literature on single-parent families found that the only situations in which children of one-parent families suffered losses of self-esteem were those in which single-parent families were stigmatized.

Such stigmatization remains widespread, even among people who should know something about the effects of self-fulfilling prophecies. Teachers shown a videotape of a child engaging in a variety of actions consistently rate the child much more negatively on a wide range of dimensions when they are told that he or she comes from a single-parent family than when they believe the child comes from an intact family. And even though serious antisocial behavior is overwhelmingly related to economic circumstances rather than to family form, children from one-parent families are far more likely to be arrested and prosecuted for the same offenses for which children from two-parent families are released to their parents.

In other words, the main policy recommendation of the new family-values crusaders would exacerbate the problems they hope to solve. Multiplying the stigmas against single parents may deter some couples from divorce or prevent some women from having babies out of wedlock, but it's unlikely to reverse the larger trend toward the declining centrality of lifelong marriage. Nor will it help the millions of children who, for better or worse, are already in one-parent families. In the real world, only 50.8% of all youths live with both biological parents; 24% live in one-parent families; 21.1% live in stepfamilies.

There Is No Perfect Family Structure

I am in favor of educating parents about the potential problems associated with divorce and rearing children alone. But we need to reject the false notion that there is one perfect family form that automatically protects children, while others automatically put them at risk. We should choose more sensitive and delicate tools than the blunt instruments that the family-values crusade employs in its effort to hammer all families into one mold. In addition to grasping the historical variability of family life, we must analyze the individual strengths, weaknesses, resources, and vulnerabilities of today's diverse families in light of their particular circumstances. Different family structures tend to produce different stress points, but ultimately it is the processes families develop within their different structures that count most in determining the outcomes for family members.

Single Mothers Can Raise Successful Children

Critical as it may be to encourage fathers to nurture their families, there needs to be an acknowledgment that the alternative is not necessarily damnation. Understanding what permits many single mothers to raise successful children may be every bit as important as understanding the power of paternal love.

Ellis Cose, *Newsweek*, October 31, 1994.

Take the male breadwinner/female homemaker model. In an economy in which work, home, and school are in different locations, this form potentially provides children with more time, more supervision, and more help with homework; the mother has more chances to meet with teachers, help out in the schools, and chauffeur children to extracurricular activities. This family structure seems to be especially beneficial to the health and happiness of men, so long as they can live up to their provider role. Yet these families often isolate the mother and lower her self-esteem. Homemakers with young children, for example, tend to be more depressed than other groups of women. Furthermore, such families may have a tough time adjusting to rapid economic change. Parents with strong values about male breadwinning are more likely than other parents to experience conflict and severe distress if the father faces economic setbacks or the mother has to seek a job.

Two-earner families have less family time together, and they are more likely to quarrel over housework, sometimes to the point of rupture. Yet Arlie Hochschild's study of two-earner couples found that both men and women were happiest in marriages that had worked out egalitarian relations. Furthermore, families with a working mother are more likely to raise children who respect women—no small advantage in a world in which women are rapidly becoming the majority of the workforce and old-fashioned notions of women's place are a potent cause of workplace hostilities.

THE ILLUSION OF HEALTHY TWO-PARENT FAMILIES

Both types of two-parent families have the potential advantage that more than one adult is available to the child. Parents can back each other up with regard to discipline, compensate for each other's weaknesses, spell each other in tasks and time, and model healthy conflict resolution or negotiation. On the other hand, this potential is not always fulfilled. Many two-parent families have the illusion that a father's presence provides them with some magic psychological shield. This attitude may lead the mother to avoid confronting damaging paternal behavior rather than risk a split. Other traditional families have fathers who are effectively absent, and therapist Deborah Luepnitz has remarked that such an unacknowledged or ambiguous loss may in the long run be more difficult to grieve than a sharp break.

Children stuck in high-conflict marriages or ones in which a father is angry and withdrawn often have worse long-term problems than children in single-parent families. One recent study of adolescent self-esteem found no differences by family structure. However, the lowest self-esteem of all groups was found in teens of two-parent families whose fathers had low levels of interest in them. Such youngsters, lacking even the excuse of the father's absence to explain his disengagement, were more likely to blame themselves for their father's lack of interest. It is also more possible for two-parent families to hide problems of abuse, incest, and alcoholism from the outside world than it is for one-parent families.

Even harmonious couples need to beware of certain pitfalls. Thinking themselves complete and self-sufficient, they may not give their children enough exposure to experiences and values that differ from their own. Such families occasionally foster an inward orientation that hinders a child from striking out in new directions or learning to appreciate difference in others. I was raised in neighborhoods in which all adults felt free to act parentally toward everyone's children, and I have noticed that, when I continue this tradition by commenting on something dangerous or hurtful that local children may be doing, some youths from two-parent families are the most hostile in their response: "You can't tell me that; you're not my mom."

POTENTIAL ADVANTAGES OF SINGLE-PARENT FAMILIES

Single-parent families have only one parent in the home to provide financial and emotional resources. When one adult is sad or angry, the whole household is upset; it takes single-parent families longer to recover from economic reverses. These are serious handicaps. Yet in many communities, female-headed families were historically an adaptive way of compensating for high male unemployment and persistent poverty. For example, an African American colleague of mine has described how his single mother's very lack of a stable marriage gave her the flexibility to link him up with a huge network of matrilineal kin and fictive cousins. She moved him in with whatever friends or relatives were employed or had contacts with successful men in the black community. He thus gained access to mentoring that his own irregularly employed (though never entirely absent) father could not provide. Today, my friend argues, the cutbacks in social programs, the growth of unemployment, and the increasing isolation of poor inner-city blacks from job networks make single motherhood less likely to be such an adaptive coping mechanism. Yet the community collapse that makes single motherhood more difficult also increases its likelihood, and heaping more guilt on the mothers does not help.

Adults in single-parent families spend less time supervising homework or interacting with teachers than adults in two-parent families, an obvious drawback. But they also spend more time talking with their children, a behavior that can lead to accelerated cognitive development and emotional empathy, so long as the parent takes care not to confide too much anger or distress. (Ironically, children of mothers who have made a conscious choice to be single and do not go through the intense grief and bitterness of a failed relationship have a potential advantage here.) In addition, adolescents in single-parent families face fewer pressures to conform to traditional gender roles. They tend to have greater maturity and feelings of efficacy than teens in two-parent families. Depending on the dynamics of the family, these characteristics can lead to more risk-taking or to more breadth and depth of thinking—or to both. In terms of academics, the absence of a father tends to be associated with lower mathematics achievement for boys but higher verbal skills. Yet the average math deficit is just as great for boys in two-parent families with low paternal involvement—a point that again directs our attention to family processes rather than family structures.

Single parents are less likely to pressure their children into social conformity and more likely to praise good grades than are parents in two-parent households—both of these, behaviors that tend to produce higher academic performance. Here single-parent families have a potential advantage over many two-parent families. But single parents are more likely to get upset and angry when their children receive bad grades, a reaction that encourages defiance and a further decline in grades.

All these variables are further complicated by the fact that they play out differently according to the race, class, and ethnicity of the family; they also have different impacts on children depending on their age, sex, individual temperament, and interaction with siblings. The negative impacts of single parenthood, interestingly, tend to be greatest among groups whose cultural values most emphasize two-parent families and paternal authority and least among those who have a history of tolerance and support for single mothers. Sara McLanahan and Gary Sandefur found that family disruption is most likely to produce harmful effects among Hispanics and least likely to do so among blacks, with whites falling in between.

ARE CHILDREN IN STEPFAMILIES AT RISK?

The contradictory data on stepfamilies also illustrate the problem with overgeneralization. While remarriage tends to reduce the stresses associated with poverty and economic insecurity, some studies suggest that, taken as a whole, children in stepfamilies face the same added risks of emotional problems as do children in one-parent families; they are actually more likely to repeat a grade than are children of never-married mothers. Yet in a recent long-term, ongoing government study, 80% of children in stepfamilies were judged to be doing well psychologically, compared to 90% in intact biological families.

Numerous researchers have suggested that girls have more problems in stepfamilies than boys, yet one recent study found not more problems for girls but merely more articulated worries. Researchers Andrew Cherlin and Frank Furstenberg point out that "stepfamilies are even less alike as a group than are nuclear families." They also cite "tremendous variation in the way parents manage the transition" to a blended family. The lack of norms and support systems for such transitions, rather than the family form itself, probably accounts for most of the problems observed in stepfamilies.

Different family forms experience different stress points over time as well. The period of greatest stress for two-parent families is generally the first few years after the birth of a child—sometimes because the husband resents his wife's transfer of time, energy, and services to the infant; sometimes because the wife resents the father's lack of such transfer. Interestingly, considerable anecdotal evidence indicates that unwed mothers with flexible jobs and financial security experience less stress during the early months, because the mother does not have to balance two relationships and two sets of needs.

The greatest period of stress for single-parent families occurs in the early teen years, when youngsters begin to demand more freedom from parental control. It's easier to wear a parent down when she or he has no ally to help resist a child's insistence that "everybody else's parents" say it's okay. Thus single parents are apt to relinquish parental decision-making prerogatives too early, a behavior that encourages negative forms of deviance in children. However, this problem can be almost entirely eliminated when another adult joins the household on a stable basis, whether that adult is a relative, a lover, or a friend. . . .

THE NEED FOR ADJUSTMENT

Children today are a precious and threatened resource. They make up only 26% of the population, and they are the poorest of any age group in the nation. Yet it is these children—not just our own children, but all children—who will grow up to appreciate the work we leave behind, to provide for the elderly (us!), to contribute to the Social Security fund on which we all depend. Either that or they will not do any of these things. It is up to all of us, not just to parents, to decide which it will be, because we are all affected by the way these children turn out.

We cannot return to "traditional" family forms and expectations that were at least partly mythical in the first place.

To help our children move successfully into the 21st century we need to stop organizing our institutions and values around the notion that every family can—or should—have one adult totally available at work and another totally available at home. We have to adjust our economic programs, schools, work policies, expectations of family life, and moral reasoning to the realities of family diversity and the challenges of global transformation. The new family-values crusade, no matter how sincere the motives of its participants, points us backward rather than forward.

"Adult society keeps many young people in emotional and mental turmoil by sending them mixed signals about important moral, ethical and legal issues."

INCONSISTENT MESSAGES ABOUT MORALITY PUT TEENS AT RISK

Edward Grimsley

In the following viewpoint, Edward Grimsley contends that adults put teens at risk by subjecting them to mixed messages about moral issues such as using illegal drugs and having sex. Grimsley asserts that adults are shirking their duty to be constructive role models for children, thereby causing confusion among teens about what is acceptable behavior. Grimsley is a nationally syndicated columnist.

As you read, consider the following questions:
1. How are adults hypocritical on the issue of illegal drugs, according to Grimsley?
2. In the author's opinion, what mixed signals do adults send about sex?
3. According to the author, how do the media promote society's hypocrisy about sexual values?

Reprinted from Edward Grimsley, "Mixed Signals to an Embattled Generation," The Washington Times, July 28, 1996, by permission of Edward Grimsley and Creators Syndicate.

Upstanding adult citizens everywhere rail against the young who commit crimes against society, but society is committing one of the most heinous crimes of all against the young.

This nation's grown men and women who are supposed to serve as constructive role models for the young are, instead, engaging in child abuse by subjecting them to acute moral, social and psychological pain and suffering.

One man who is concerned about what the adult society of America is doing to the young is Dr. George R. Holmes, a noted child psychiatrist. A recent *Washington Times* article quoted him as saying modern teen-agers and even pre-adolescents "are experiencing a wide variety of negative influences that no previous generation has had to confront." The results include "higher rates of delinquency, psychiatric illness and deaths among teen-agers."

ADULTS SEND MIXED MESSAGES TO YOUTH

Contemporary news stories seemed to confirm Dr. Holmes' theory. They made it distressingly clear that adult society keeps many young people in emotional and mental turmoil by sending them mixed signals about important moral, ethical and legal issues.

One such issue is the use of illegal drugs. Over and over, adults warn children that they flirt with disaster by such acts as smoking joints and snorting cocaine. Drug users, say the adults, will disgrace themselves and their families, incur the wrath of the law and imperil their livelihoods.

Every day, the law does indeed punish many ordinary young people from ordinary neighborhoods for using illegal drugs. Many have gone to jail merely for possessing a single marijuana joint.

But the young can learn from news stories that some people who use illegal drugs and admit it get cushy jobs in the White House. One even became president of the United States. It's true that President Bill Clinton insists he never inhaled, but American anti-drug laws do not stipulate that a user must inhale to commit an illegal act. Mr. Clinton violated the law simply by holding a joint.

Also from news stories the young learn that some people who are charged with the most serious drug offenses go not to prison but back to their football teams to continue to earn bundles of money. Oh, these privileged individuals may have to vacuum a few hospital room floors and perform other community services over a period of time, but most young people who are behind bars on drug charges would much prefer that kind of "punishment" to time in prison.

CONFLICTING SIGNALS ABOUT SEX CONFUSE TEENS

Conflicting signals like these make it difficult for the young to know whether using drugs will bring them punishment, disgrace and ruin, or rewards, prestige and success.

Possibly even more confusing are the signals adult society sends about sex. It admonishes the young to abstain from sex outside marriage, and in some instances even threatens to put them in jail if they don't.

That's happening in Gem County, Idaho. To discourage unwed teen-agers from getting pregnant, County Prosecutor Douglas Varie has begun to charge those who do and their boyfriends with violating the state's law against fornication.

That Mr. Varie's objective is laudable is undebatable. But is he in fairness also enforcing the anti-fornication law against unmarried adults? Young people who read the news stories about his actions will find no indication he is raiding the motels and hotels of his area in search of trysting grown-ups.

THE LOSS OF MORAL STANDARDS

One reason why so many young people are having sex is the loss of objective moral standards. Their models are adults who abandon integrity about as quickly as they abandon their spouses. In one generation, we have passed from the free distribution of *Gideon Bibles* to the free distribution of condoms.

Cal Thomas, *Conservative Chronicle*, October 15, 1997.

But young readers could learn from another story that while Gem County's adult prosecutor is punishing teen-agers for fornication, the adults who run the Army are doing nothing to prevent it. At least 70 American soldiers in Bosnia have become pregnant since the peacekeeping mission began in December 1995, yet the Army has punished not a single woman or her boyfriend for engaging in illicit sex.

While it restricts the consumption of alcoholic beverages and cigarettes, the Army has no ban on sexual relations between unmarried couples—unless one is an officer and the other is an enlisted man or woman. Then the Army might punish them for violating its prohibition on fraternization between social unequals.

This suggests that teen-agers in Idaho who wish to engage in illicit sex should join the Army first.

The Hypocrisy of Adults

In addition to these particular conflicting stories about sex, there are stories about famous adults who engage in sex with people to whom they are not married: princes, princesses, movie stars, television performers, politicians and other VIPs. Instead of jailing these violators of the laws against illicit sex, society seems to condone their conduct.

It is too bad the young cannot sue America's adult society for damages for sending such hypocritical signals about right and wrong. Hitting grown-ups in their wallet might induce them to be more honest in making and enforcing the rules of life.

> "*A heightened anger toward homosexuals, plain conservative values on the parts of parents, and a general malaise for homosexuals . . . either forces or drives these youths to the street.*"

GAY TEENS ARE AT RISK

Rosemarie Buchanan

Rosemarie Buchanan asserts in the following viewpoint that gay teens are at risk of becoming homeless because they are sometimes rejected or cast out by family members. Furthermore, the author maintains, gay teens are more likely to abuse drugs or alcohol in response to feelings of alienation. Buchanan is a writer based in Chicago.

As you read, consider the following questions:

1. What percentage of youths at the Outside In homeless shelter classify themselves as gay, according to Buchanan?
2. Why is it difficult to estimate how many homeless teens are gay, in Buchanan's view?
3. In the author's opinion, why do some gay teens seek the streets?

Excerpted from Rosemarie Buchanan, "Young, Homeless, and Gay," *Human Rights*, Winter 1995, ©1995 American Bar Association. Reprinted with permission.

The teenager had nowhere to go, except to join the growing numbers like him who have taken to living on the streets. He was lucky, however, and found Terry Person, program director for Community United Against Violence, a service agency for homeless youth in San Francisco. Speaking about the boy, Person says, "He's an unusual case because he came to San Francisco with parental permission. He came from Kansas and stayed with friends, then found himself on the street."

Person is talking about a gay teen whose parents kicked him out of his family because of his sexuality.

While statistics are scant, it is now believed that a disproportionate number of gay and lesbian teens can be found among the country's homeless population.

Some shelters, like Person's, are struggling to help, either by offering counseling or providing critical job training. Their programs can be seen as models for other agencies or shelters facing this issue.

OUTCAST BY THEIR FAMILIES

These teens are homeless not by choice, but because they are no longer welcome within their families.

A case study performed on a social service agency for young people in Oregon illustrates what social workers see day to day in their dealings with young street people: Many of them are gay, are unsure of their sexuality or are confused about their identity.

Some say a heightened anger toward homosexuals, plain conservative values on the parts of parents, and a general malaise for homosexuals in our society either forces or drives these youths to the street.

HOW MANY HOMELESS YOUTH ARE GAY?

David Allen, a lawyer in Portland, Oregon, analyzed data collected by Outside In, a medical and counseling agency serving homeless young people. Allen is one of the shelter's former board members.

According to the agency's findings, about 20 percent of Outside In's clients classified themselves as gay, lesbian or bisexual as of 1993. During the following year, that number increased to 30 percent.

A nationwide sex survey published by the University of Chicago estimated that 3 percent of men surveyed designated themselves as homosexual and about 1.5 percent of female respondents said they were lesbian. In these terms, the number of homosexual youth at Outside In is at least 10 times the average.

In addition, the Outside In study found that 9 percent at the Portland shelter classify themselves as "unsure" of their sexual identity.

"And even that figure may be low," Allen contends. "Seventy-one percent of respondents characterize themselves as heterosexual, but there is undeniably a greater incentive to adopt the latter rather than the former label. An unknown number of 'straight' respondents are probably more accurately characterized as 'unsure' at best.". . .

An Explosive Issue for Families

At Community United Against Violence, Person believes that many gay and lesbian youths end up in shelters because of their identity problems.

"They come out to their parents and get kicked out, or are in the coming-out process and start exhibiting," she says. "They don't know why they feel uncomfortable, but it leads to family conflict."

Allen agrees. "Homosexuality is an explosive issue for many families, an issue which can be resolved in the short term by expulsion of the 'disruptive' child from the family circle. Young people with acute sexual-identity crisis are likely to abuse drugs or alcohol out of frustration and/or alienation; chronic substance abuse in turn precipitates family breakup."

To help gay and lesbian homeless teens, Community United Against Violence chiefly provides job search assistance, believing that these youths are in a transition time. While they are discovering their sexuality, what they really need is to move back into society through employment.

Another shelter, the Larkin Street Youth Center in San Francisco, deals with more dire problems, offering intensive counseling to deal with immediate problems of prostitution and drug abuse.

"I think the proportion of gay and lesbian youth is very high [out of] the ones we see here," says Leslie Laughlin, who works at Larkin. "A lot of it has to do with their coming out. Once they get to be about 13, they're thrown out. It's 'Hit the road; go to San Francisco.'"

Allen contends that teens who express uncertainty about their sexuality are both pushed and pulled toward the street.

"Sexual minority youth from small towns and cities or conservative regions frequently find adolescence a living hell," he believes. "They become the victims of a cycle of diminished expectations. They may not only be pushed from the home; they may be 'pulled' to the street as the road toward the realization of self."

"Survival Sex"

Laughlin adds that many homeless under the age of 15 engage in "survival sex" because they can't get a minimum wage job, which doesn't automatically classify them as gay or lesbian.

"They may be doing what it takes to get the money to live, and not be gay or lesbian, but just very practical and desperate," says Patricia Hanrahan, director of the American Bar Association's (ABA) Commission on Homelessness and Poverty.

"There are men who have sex with men because it's simply something they do," says Mark Agrast, senior legislative assistant for Congressman Jerry Studds. "That kind of thing is an empirical problem with kids who may be gay," adds Agrast, who is also a former chair of the Rights of Lesbians and Gay Men committee of the ABA's Section of Individual Rights & Responsibilities.

Coming Out to Families Can Be Dangerous

[Gay, lesbian, and bisexual youth] get kicked out of homes, abused, and disowned; parents refuse to speak to their child or force them to seek "reparative" therapy. While coming out can indeed be liberating—and for some people is a necessity to maintain their sanity—for young people still emotionally and financially dependent on their parents, it can all too often be a dangerous thing.

Laura Lorenzen, *In the Family*, January 1998.

Because few studies have been done on the issue of gay homeless teens, quantitative information is hard to come by on the subject. The Hedric-Martin Institute, which is the largest social service agency for gay and lesbian youth, estimates that at least 40 to 50 percent of the homeless population in New York City is composed of gay or lesbian teens.

Andy Humm, policy coordinator for the New York–based institute, said statistically, this population is difficult to define. Many youth may cast themselves as heterosexual while performing homosexual acts.

Based on the center's experience, Humm suggested that about 26 percent of gay and lesbian youths leave home, and many of those end up on the streets. They are then frequently exposed to sexually transmitted diseases, from both sexual partners and drug abuse.

Why Do Some Gay Teens Seek the Streets?

At Outside In, roughly 67 percent of the clients admit to using alcohol and/or drugs, possibly as a result of feeling out of place in society and within their families. It's possible that teens seek the streets to support a drug habit.

But Allen believes the streets offer even a more substantial pull: validation of the kids' identity.

"The streets may be the first place a young gay or lesbian experiences validation," Allen notes. On the streets, gay males not only publicly identify as gay—a critical prerequisite to other developmental tasks of adolescence—but also get paid for it through prostitution. As harmful as that may be in the long run, in the short run they are receiving rewards and approvals, and joining a community," Allen adds.

All is not bleak for these teens, however. Person's organization helps move teens from the shelter to society through job training programs. Although a disproportionate number of homosexual or uncertain teens make their way to the streets, it doesn't mean they will stay there.

PERIODICAL BIBLIOGRAPHY

The following articles have been selected to supplement the diverse views presented in this chapter. Addresses are provided for periodicals not indexed in the *Readers' Guide to Periodical Literature*, the *Alternative Press Index*, the *Social Sciences Index*, or the *Index to Legal Periodicals and Books*.

Nell Bernstein	"Learning to Love," *Mother Jones*, January/February 1995.
Mona Charen	"How to Raise a Killer," *Conservative Chronicle*, June 18, 1997. Available from PO Box 37077, Boone, IA 50037-0077.
Alexander Cockburn	"The War on Kids," *Nation*, June 3, 1996.
Greg Donaldson	"Throwaway Youth," *New York Times*, July 3, 1994.
Bettyann H. Kevles and Daniel J. Kevles	"Scapegoat Biology," *Discover*, October 1997.
Mike Males	"Poverty, Rape, Adult/Teen Sex: Why 'Pregnancy Prevention' Programs Don't Work," *Phi Delta Kappan*, January 1994.
Bronwyn Mayden	"Child Sexual Abuse: Teen Pregnancy's Silent Partner," *Children's Voice*, Winter 1996. Available from Child Welfare League of America, 440 First St. NW, 3rd Fl., Washington, DC 20001-2085.
David Popenoe	"A World Without Fathers," *Wilson Quarterly*, Spring 1996.
Karen S. Schneider	"Mission Impossible," *People Weekly*, June 3, 1996.
Joseph P. Shapiro and Missy Daniel	"Teenage Wasteland?" *U.S. News & World Report*, October 23, 1995.
Arlene Skolnick and Stacey Rosencrantz	"The New Crusade for the Old Family," *American Prospect*, Summer 1994.
Norman Solmon	"'Teen People' and the Souls of Young Folks," *Liberal Opinion Week*, January 26, 1998. Available from PO Box 880, Vinton, IA 52349-0880.
Charlene Marmer Solomon	"Latchkey Kids," *Parents*, March 1994.
Ruby Takanishi and Jane Sims Podesta	"Years of Wonder—and Risk," *People Weekly*, November 13, 1995.
M. Witwer	"Early Sexual Activity, but Not Childhood Sexual Abuse, Increases the Odds of Teenage Pregnancy," *Family Planning Perspectives*, July 1, 1997. Available from the Alan Guttmacher Institute, 120 Wall St., New York, NY 10005.

HOW CAN SOCIETY DEAL WITH TEENAGE CRIME AND VIOLENCE?

CHAPTER PREFACE

In March 1998, the U.S. Department of Education released a report showing that 47 percent of public schools reported at least one serious or nonviolent crime during the 1996–97 school year. Another 10 percent reported at least one serious violent crime. The problem of school violence persists, as indicated by a string of fatal shootings that took place during the 1997–98 school year. In all, over a dozen people were shot to death and more than forty people were wounded. Of the suspects in the shootings, almost all were teenagers, while one was an eleven-year-old.

The deadly attacks have prompted many people to wonder if and how schools can be made safer. Some observers assert that the answer is in limiting the access these teenagers and preteens have to guns. In an editorial in *USA Today* following the Arkansas tragedy, in which four students and a teacher were killed and ten others wounded, Jonathan Kellerman criticized a culture that teaches children how to hunt and use guns. "Handing a frightfully immature, troubled human being a firearm and encouraging him to stalk and kill animals is beyond absurd," he wrote. Laws that restrict juvenile access to guns have gained support in recent years. As of this writing, fifteen states hold adults criminally liable if they do not keep loaded guns inaccessible to children or if they do not use a gun lock. Similar federal legislation has been proposed in Congress.

Other people contend that access to guns is not at fault, asserting that poor parenting is the cause of these crimes. An editorial by Zach Myles in the University of Virginia's student newspaper concluded, "Blaming juvenile violence on lax gun control laws and television violence is a copout. Americans regularly express that sentiment, however, giving would-be parents an excuse for raising dishonorable children. In fact, the real blame should rest on those who hold responsibility to mold the child—his parents."

Whether the cause is inadequate parenting, too many guns, or other factors, incidents of teen violence have led to various proposed solutions to this problem. Ways to reduce teenage crime and violence, in the schools and elsewhere, are considered by the authors in the following chapter.

| "Detaining a rapist or murderer in a juvenile facility until the age of 18 or 21 isn't even a slap on the hand."

VIOLENT JUVENILE CRIMINALS SHOULD BE TREATED AS ADULTS

Linda J. Collier

Violent crimes by youths, such as the 1998 school shooting in Jonesboro, Arkansas, in which four students and one teacher were killed, point to a need to treat some juvenile criminals as adults, argues Linda J. Collier in the following viewpoint. She asserts that the juvenile justice system is outdated because it was designed to deal with the vandals and petty thieves of an earlier era, not today's juvenile murderers and rapists. Collier, a Pennsylvania lawyer who has worked in Philadelphia's juvenile court, maintains that the states should set a uniform minimum age for trying violent youths as adults.

As you read, consider the following questions:

1. How much has crime by juveniles increased since 1984, according to statistics cited by Collier?
2. According to the author, what is the operating principle of juvenile adjudications?
3. In Collier's view, what is one reason for the lack of consistency in waiver laws?

Reprinted from Linda J. Collier, "Doing Adult Time for an Adult Crime," The Washington Post National Weekly Edition, April 6, 1998, by permission of the author.

When prosecutor Brent Davis said he wasn't sure if he could charge 11-year-old Andrew Golden and 13-year-old Mitchell Johnson as adults after the slaughter on March 24, 1998, in Jonesboro, Arkansas, I cringed. But not for the reasons you might think. I knew he was formulating a judgment based on laws that have not had a major overhaul for more than 100 years. I knew his hands were tied by the long-standing creed that juvenile offenders, generally defined as those under the age of 18, are to be treated rather than punished. I knew he would have to do legal cartwheels to get the case out of the juvenile system. But most of all, I cringed because today's juvenile suspects—even those who are accused of committing the most violent crimes—are still regarded by the law as children first and criminals second.

JUVENILE CRIME HAS INCREASED

As astonishing as the Jonesboro events were, this is hardly the first time that children with access to guns and other weapons have brought tragedy to a school. Only weeks before the Jonesboro shootings, three girls in Paducah, Kentucky, were killed in their school lobby when a 14-year-old classmate allegedly opened fire on them. Authorities said he had several guns with him, and the alleged murder weapon was one of seven stolen from a neighbor's garage. And the day after the Jonesboro shootings, a 14-year-old in Daly City, California, was charged as a juvenile after he allegedly fired at his middle-school principal with a semiautomatic handgun.

It's not a new or unusual phenomenon for children to commit violent crimes at younger and younger ages, but it often takes a shocking incident to draw our attention to a trend already in progress. According to the U.S. Department of Justice, crimes committed by juveniles have increased by 60 percent since 1984. Where juvenile delinquency was once limited to truancy or vandalism, juveniles now are more likely to be the perpetrators of serious and deadly crimes such as arson, aggravated assault, rape and murder. And these violent offenders increasingly include those as young as the Jonesboro suspects. Since 1965, the number of 12-year-olds arrested for violent crimes has doubled and the number of 13- and 14-year-olds has tripled, according to government statistics.

Those statistics are a major reason why we need to revamp our antiquated juvenile justice system. Nearly every state, including Arkansas, has laws that send most youthful violent offenders to the juvenile courts, where they can only be found "delinquent" and confined in a juvenile facility (typically not past age 21). In recent years, many states have enacted changes in their juvenile crime laws, and some have lowered the age at which a juvenile can be tried as an adult for certain violent crimes. Virginia, for example, has reduced its minimum age to 14, and suspects accused of murder and aggravated malicious wounding are automatically waived to adult court. Illinois is now sending some 13-year-olds to adult court after a hearing in juvenile court. In Kansas, a 1996 law allows juveniles as young as 10 to be prosecuted as adults in some cases. These are steps in the right direction, but too many states still treat violent offenders under 16 as juveniles who belong in the juvenile system.

PERSONAL EXPERIENCES

My views are not those of a frustrated prosecutor. I have represented children as a court-appointed guardian *ad litem*, or temporary guardian, in the Philadelphia juvenile justice system. Loosely defined, a guardian ad litem is responsible for looking after the best interest of a neglected or rebellious child who has come into the juvenile courts. It is often a humbling experience as I try to help children whose lives have gone awry, sometimes because of circumstances beyond their control.

My experience has made me believe that the system is doing a poor job at treatment as well as punishment. One of my "girls," a chronic truant, was a foster child who longed to be adopted. She often talked of how she wanted a pink room, a frilly bunk bed and sisters with whom she could share her dreams. She languished in foster care from age 2 to 13 because her drug-ravaged mother would not relinquish her parental rights. Initially, the girl refused to tolerate the half-life that the state had maintained was in her best interest. But as it became clear that we would never persuade her mother to give up her rights, the girl became a frequent runaway. Eventually she ended up pregnant, wandering from place to place and committing adult crimes to survive. No longer a child, not quite a woman, she is the kind of teenage offender for whom the juvenile system has little or nothing to offer.

A brief history: Proceedings in juvenile justice began in 1890 in Chicago, where the original mandate was to save wayward children and protect them from the ravages of society. The system called for children to be processed through an appendage of the family court. By design, juveniles were to be kept away from the court's criminal side, the district attorney and adult correctional institutions.

By race, ethnicity, community, and whether respondent is a crime victim, United States, 1994[a]

Question: "In your view, should juveniles who commit violent crimes be treated the same as adults, or should they be given more lenient treatment in a juvenile court?"

	Treated the same as adults	Given more lenient treatment	Treated tougher[b]	Depends[b]	Don't know
National	68%	13%	[c]	16%	3%
Race, ethnicity					
White	69	12	[c]	16	3
Black	71	17	[c]	11	1
Hispanic	64	15	[c]	19	2
Community					
City	70	7	1	17	5
Suburb	68	15	[c]	16	1
Small town	66	17	[c]	16	1
Rural area	69	14	[c]	15	2
Victim of crime	71	8	1	15	5

[a] Percents may not add to 100 because of rounding.

[b] Response volunteered.

[c] Less than 0.5 percent.

Source: Bureau of Justice Statistics, *Sourcebook of Criminal Justice Statistics 1994*.

Typically, initial procedures are informal, non-threatening and not open to public scrutiny. A juvenile suspect is interviewed by an "intake" officer who determines the child's fate. The intake officer may issue a warning, lecture and release; he may detain the suspect; or, he may decide to file a petition, subjecting the child to juvenile "adjudication" proceedings. If the law allows, the intake officer may make a recommendation that the juvenile be transferred to adult criminal court.

AN OUTDATED SYSTEM

An adjudication is similar to a hearing, rather than a trial, although the juvenile may be represented by counsel and a juvenile prosecutor will represent the interests of the community. It is important to note that throughout the proceedings, no matter which side of the fence the parties are on, the operating principle is that everyone is working in the best interests of the child. Juvenile court judges do not issue findings of guilt, but decide whether a child is delinquent. If delinquency is found, the judge must decide the child's fate. Should the child be sent back to the family—assuming there is one? Declare him or her "in need of supervision," which brings in the intense help of social services? Remove the child from the family and place him or her in foster care? Confine the child to a state institution for juvenile offenders?

This system was developed with truants, vandals and petty thieves in mind. But this model is not appropriate for the violent juvenile offender of today. Detaining a rapist or murderer in a juvenile facility until the age of 18 or 21 isn't even a slap on the hand. If a juvenile is accused of murdering, raping or assaulting someone with a deadly weapon, the suspect should automatically be sent to adult criminal court. What's to ponder?

With violent crime becoming more prevalent among the junior set, it's a mystery why there hasn't been a major overhaul of juvenile justice laws long before now. Will the Jonesboro shootings be the incident that makes us take a hard look at the current system? When it became evident that the early release of Jesse Timmendequas—whose murder of 7-year-old Megan Kanka in New Jersey sparked national outrage—had caused unwarranted tragedy, legislative action was swift. Now New Jersey has Megan's Law, which requires the advance notification of a sexual predator's release into a neighborhood. Other states have followed suit.

It is unequivocally clear that the same type of mandate is needed to establish a uniform minimum age for trying juveniles as adults. As it stands now, there is no consistency in state laws governing waivers to adult court. One reason for this lack of uniformity is the absence of direction from the federal government or Congress. The Bureau of Justice Statistics reports that adjacent states such as New York and Pennsylvania respond differently to 16-year-old criminals, with New York tending to treat offenders of that age as adults and Pennsylvania handling them in the juvenile justice system.

THE LONG-TERM SOLUTION

Federal prosecution of juveniles is not totally unheard of, but it is uncommon. The Bureau of Justice Statistics estimates that during 1994, at least 65 juveniles were referred to the attorney general for transfer to adult status. In such cases, the U.S. attorney's office must certify a substantial federal interest in the case and show that one of the following is true: The state does not have jurisdiction; the state refuses to assume jurisdiction or the state does not have adequate services for juvenile offenders; the offense is a violent felony, drug trafficking or firearm offense as defined by the U.S. Code.

Exacting hurdles, but not insurmountable. In the Jonesboro case, prosecutor Davis has been exploring ways to enlist the federal court's jurisdiction. Whatever happens, federal prosecutions of young offenders are clearly not the long-term answer. The states must act. As far as I can see, the next step is clear: Children who knowingly engage in adult conduct and adult crimes should automatically be subject to adult rules and adult prison time.

| "We seem almost always to respond to teenagers with an authoritarianism in the name of clarity and standards."

JUVENILE CRIMINALS SHOULD NOT BE TREATED AS ADULTS

William Ayers

Trying youths as adults is a faulty approach to juvenile crime, contends William Ayers in the following viewpoint. Ayers argues that juveniles placed in adult prisons are more likely to be sexually assaulted, to commit suicide, and to return to crime after they are released. He asserts that a more appropriate approach to juvenile crime is to provide young people with better educational and employment opportunities. Ayers is a professor of education and a university scholar at the University of Illinois at Chicago. He is also the author of *A Kind and Just Parent: The Children of Juvenile Court.*

As you read, consider the following questions:

1. According to Ayers, what is the "schizophrenic view of children"?
2. Why has youth murder increased, in the author's opinion?
3. Why do "zero tolerance" policies cause neglect, according to Ayers?

Reprinted from William Ayers, "The Criminalization of Youth," *Rethinking Schools*, Winter 1997/1998, by permission of the author.

Our culture embraces a schizophrenic view of children: We romance childhood as a time of innocence and beauty, and we simultaneously construct an image of original sin and elemental evil lurking in those little bodies. Children are angels and devils—pure and wicked, clean and corrupt, lambs and devils. When children are left to themselves, however, our culture assumes the demon child has the upper hand. *The Exorcist* and *Village of the Damned* are popular manifestations, *The Lord of the Flies* its most enduring expression. Young people today find themselves in a peculiarly precarious landscape—reified as consumers, demonized as a threat, they inhabit a cultural fault-line that is bumpy for all and fatal for some.

A HOPELESS VIEW OF YOUTH

While these contradictions have been a part of our culture for over a century (before the Victorian age, children were miniature adults and the goal was to grow up as quickly as possible), a more hopeless view of children and adolescence is now taking hold. What is more, this view is backed by legislative proposals such as trying more children and teens as adults, building more youth prisons, and codifying the "three strikes and you're out" approach even for children.

An ominous new language of bestiality and disease has gained popularity to describe particular young people as unlike any we have ever known. "Violent juvenile crime is a national epidemic," declares Rep. Bill McCollum (R-FL), and "today's superpredators are feral, presocial beings with no sense of right and wrong." Over time the rhetoric takes hold. As Michael Doring wrote in the spring of 1997 in *The Chicago Tribune*, "The political consensus developing in favor of fundamental national changes in juvenile justice comes down to this: A child stops being a child when he picks up a gun."

Rep. McCollum declares that "the really bad news" is that "America will experience a 31% increase in teenagers" in coming years. The kids themselves are the trouble. Among them, he says, are "the highly crime-prone males—teen-agers from fatherless homes growing up in neighborhoods where gangs, drugs and violence are commonplace and consequences for misbehavior are almost nonexistent." McCollum insists that the threat is palpable: "A juvenile who commits cold-blooded murder can be walking in your neighborhood in less than a year."

Rep. McCollum is backing up his rhetoric with legislative clout. He has proposed the Juvenile Crime Control Act of 1997 (originally called the Superpredator Incapacitation Act) which calls for $1.5 billion in incentive grants to states to encourage automatic transfers to adult courts for juveniles charged with certain crimes, escalating predetermined punishment for repeat juvenile offenders, as well as sanctions for their parents, and the public release of previously sealed juvenile criminal records. With its aggregation of certain youth into a convenient and manageable mob and its one-size-fits-all simplicity, it passed the House 286-132 and moves, with the Clinton administration's support for key provisions, inexorably toward the Senate. Rep. McCollum's bill represents a decisive withdrawal from a century of difficult, uneven progress in relation to juvenile justice, undermining the fundamental thesis that a child in crisis, a child in trouble, is still a child. [As of March 1998, no action had been taken on the Senate floor.]

Rep. McCollum relies on an entirely inaccurate popular impression that youth crime is a runaway train, reckless, out of control, unpredictably dangerous, picking up speed as it careens down the track toward our town or neighborhood. We read about teenagers being "wild in the streets" and of a "ticking demographic time bomb," the 3-year-olds of today morphing overnight into tiny monsters in sneakers.

The truth is more complicated. The overwhelming majority of kids are not criminals—less than one-half of 1% of youth 10–17 are charged with violent crimes. In fact, youth crime is relatively flat over decades and juvenile arrests for violent offenses have declined dramatically since 1994. Youth murder is up, it's true, but why? Access to guns. What would have been a terrible incident twenty years ago—a brutal fight, a kid hit by another kid with a baseball bat—is now too often fatal. Today the immature, impulsive kid can get a gun.

THE TRUTH ABOUT ADOLESCENT CRIME

While each instance of youth-on-youth violence is alarming, the hidden, terrible truth is that most murder victims under 18 are killed by adults; 70% of the murderers of children in 1994 were adults, and it is six times more likely that a parent will kill his or her teenage child than the other way around.

Under Rep. McCollum's bill, we would return to the practices of the 19th century, erasing the distinctions between children and adults, thrusting youngsters into adult courts and prisons, ensuring that they are preyed upon sexually and physically, hardened and destroyed. Six in 10 juveniles tried as adults are non-violent offenders, and headline-grabbing youth crimes account for less than 1% of all juvenile delinquency. But once in adult prisons, youth are twice as likely to be beaten or to commit suicide and five times as likely to be sexually assaulted. Those who survive have higher recidivism rates than kids charged with similar offenses but kept under the supervision of juvenile courts. Ironically, McCollum-type proposals—tough-sounding but ineffective—contribute to rising crime rates.

Dan Wasserman ©1997 Boston Globe. Distributed by the Los Angeles Times Syndicate. Reprinted by permission.

Transferring children as young as 13 years old automatically to adult courts without a juvenile hearing is already creating a peculiarly American gulag for the poor in states that have vigorously pursued this approach. In Rep. McCollum's own Florida, one of the severest get-tough states, youth sentenced to adult courts return to criminal activity and commit consistently more serious crimes than their counterparts who remain under the jurisdiction of juvenile courts. Florida's approach—which denies judges the opportunity to examine the specific circumstances of each case, uncovering the particular problems and possibilities in each situation, and then opens confidential records just as disaffected young people are struggling to reintegrate into society—is an economic death sentence for many. It guarantees a growing population that is hurt, hopeless, and angry.

We seem almost always to respond to teenagers with an authoritarianism in the name of clarity and standards. For example, "zero tolerance" seems to be becoming a favorite phrase, promoted as clarifying what might have been perceived as murky, ambiguous. It's odd though: I don't have any murkiness at all on drug abuse, for example. I think cigarettes are toxic, alcohol poisonous—heavier drugs are even worse—and so I don't use them, and I strongly disapprove of their use. What does saying I have "zero tolerance" for them add? It sounds tougher, perhaps, but what would I do, for example, what action would I take if I saw someone abusing alcohol? Kill them? Jail them? Punch them out? Expel them? Sounding tough is quite a different thing from prescribing what that toughness entails. And since contexts and circumstances are always specific and often complex, wise prescriptions will likely be various.

Furthermore, saying I have "zero tolerance" for alcohol gives it an oddly privileged position. How much tolerance do I have for sexual abuse? For bigotry? Intolerance or disrespect? Meanness or thoughtlessness? Well, it's clear that these are complicated. "Zero tolerance" simplifies, closes the door to conversation. Move into more complicated issues and the need for conversation only intensifies. Young people, in particular, need steady grown-ups to talk to, to think with, to bounce back off of. Closing the door is a form of abandonment, of neglect.

SETTING LIMITS

We should refine our standard and ask, what if this were my child? The question cannot be about some abstract child, every child, the mob of children. That turns other people's children into things, objectifies them. To ask, is it good enough for my child?—not, is it a perfect arrangement for my child?—is to begin to set limits of acceptability. Personalizing our approach to juveniles does not mean that there are no serious consequences to action or behavior, but it does remind us that a child who breaks the law will return to society someday, and that among our central goals must be recovery. It reminds us that our efforts on behalf of our children and other people's children must include cleaning up their environment—removing adult-controlled toxic elements like guns and drugs—and a sustained struggle to provide productive work, decent schools, and community centers to support and challenge them, to engage their hopes and dreams and capacities. We must fight for the obvious: a child in crisis, a child in trouble, is still a child.

74

"Injunctions represent a breakthrough strategy in the effort to undermine youth street gangs."

GANG INJUNCTIONS CAN PREVENT TEENAGE VIOLENCE

Roger L. Conner

In the following viewpoint, Roger L. Conner argues that gang injunctions, court orders that prohibit gang members from performing certain activities such as congregating in specific public areas, help reduce violence. Such injunctions should be upheld by the courts, Conner maintains, despite the protests of the American Civil Liberties Union (ACLU), which claims that the orders are unconstitutional. He asserts that injunctions are an effective form of intervention that make it harder for gangs to engage in criminal activity and recruit new members. Conner is executive director of the Center for the Community Interest, a nonpartisan organization that helps citizens regain control over public spaces and defends public policies that balance community responsibility and individual liberties.

As you read, consider the following questions:

1. What approaches are needed in the antigang effort, according to Conner?
2. Why are some otherwise legal acts enjoined, according to the author?
3. According to the Supreme Court, as cited by the author, what is the only type of association that is constitutionally protected?

Reprinted from Roger L. Conner, "A Gangsta's Rights," *The Responsive Community*, Winter 1995/1996, by permission of *The Responsive Community*.

A hallmark of the U.S. Constitution is that fundamental rights extend even to those people whom many would consider the least deserving—perhaps especially to such people. But in California, a court has interpreted this principle so broadly as to prevent communities from reigning in those who make their neighborhoods unlivable.

THE BATTLE OVER GANG INJUNCTIONS

The case in question grew out of an innovative tactic, pioneered by Los Angeles District Attorney Gil Garcetti and pro bono lawyers from the law firm of Latham & Watkins. The strategy is to obtain injunctions that prohibit gang members from engaging in certain activities. The efforts have been so effective that they have been duplicated throughout the state. In San Jose, for example, residents of the Rocksprings neighborhood were constantly in fear of two violent street gangs. Gang members staked out their turf with graffiti, loud music, and urine. Gunshots and drug deals were commonplace, and car windows were frequently smashed. So in 1993, the city attorney brought a civil action to have six key gang members declared public nuisances. California District Court Judge Robert Foley sided with the district attorney and issued an injunction prohibiting the gang leaders from activities that harassed and intimidated the entire community. According to San Jose City Attorney Joan Gallo, arrests in the targeted area dropped by 72 percent in two years, and many gang-related problems were largely eliminated. As one enjoined gang member remarked, "There's nothing for me to do anymore."

But then the American Civil Liberties Union (ACLU) brought suit—and won. In *The State of California v. Carlos Acuna, et al.*, the California Court of Appeals vacated the injunction and adopted the ACLU's contention that gang members have a right to the tools and tricks of their trade. The three-judge panel held that activities such as carrying crowbars and chains, possessing "slim jims" and spray paint, engaging motorists in traffic, and climbing trees to maintain lookouts, are all constitutionally protected. The court also maintained that gang members have a right to gather together for such purposes in public places. Apparently uncompelling was the trial court's determination that, as a group, gang members used these actions as a direct means of intimidation, assault, theft, vandalism, drug dealing, and other crimes.

The California Supreme Court has agreed to review the ruling and many California jurisdictions are deeply worried about the outcome. [On January 30, 1997, the court upheld the injunction in a 4-3 ruling.] Injunctions represent a breakthrough strategy in the effort to undermine youth street gangs. The *Los Angeles Times* reported that a civil order in Burbank dissolved a gang-run drug ring entirely. In Panorama City, gang activity was reduced by 70 percent. The Los Angeles County Sheriff noted that in the six months after an injunction took effect, Norwalk police, who had been summoned to a gang-plagued neighborhood an average of eight times a day, were called only *once a month* on gang-related incidents.

The injunctions, by preventing gangsters from flaunting their gang affiliation and congregating in specified public areas, directly attack the sense of collective impunity that drives gang activity. They thus give the community the leverage it needs to face down threats of violence and rebuild a culture of respect. And while supporters admit that civil orders must be only one part of a wider anti-gang effort—an effort that would include education, youth diversion, community policing, and traditional law enforcement—they are powerful preventive tools.

The ACLU's Reasoning

The ACLU's lawyers insist that it is impermissible for a court to issue a civil order to prohibit gang members from any act that is not expressly illegal. "The issuance of injunctions makes some activities criminal that would not otherwise be criminal," said Amitai Schwartz, the ACLU lawyer challenging the San Jose order. "It's a shortcut for law enforcement [and] an end run around constitutional protections." The Court of Appeals agreed: an individual may be forbidden from illegal acts like dealing drugs, but not from anything that is ordinarily legal. In other words, gang members cannot be prohibited from brandishing heavy chains or crowbars, even when such weapons constitute an implicit threat to anyone who fails to show proper compliance.

The city attorney had countered that any activity that constitutes a public nuisance is a crime. The California Penal Code defines a public nuisance as "anything which is injurious to health, or is indecent, or is offensive to the senses, or an obstruction to the free use of property, so as to interfere with the comfortable enjoyment of life or property by an entire community, or by any considerable number of persons." The appellate court opinion in *Acuna* cited this definition but, adopting the ACLU's reasoning, narrowed the meaning of the word "anything" in the statute to apply only to "criminal activity" as defined by other statutes. Thus, the court held, any activity that could "have legitimate non-criminal purposes . . . may not be judicially enjoined."

It is this holding that most perplexes critics of the ruling. For, in fact, the law is filled with many examples of otherwise lawful acts that are enjoined because, in context, they amount to unreasonable behavior. Abusive spouses are ordered to stay a certain distance from their victims, though walking is itself hardly criminal. Playing music, yelling, and applauding are enjoined when an establishment's noise level consistently disturbs its neighbors, though at a stadium rock concert these activities are legal and encouraged. Other examples abound.

Not All Associations Are Equal

The ACLU has also used the *Acuna* case to get the courts to broaden the range of association protected by the First Amendment. It is the position of the ACLU that the First Amendment's protection of expression includes all personal association. The San Jose injunction infringes on this right, lawyers argue, by prohibiting gang members from congregating on the four square blocks they call their turf—where, incidentally, not one of them lives. Adopting this view, the California appeals panel stated that "non-criminal associational conduct cannot be enjoined solely on the basis of [gang] membership."

The Court's Explanation

No appeal to freedoms of speech or association warrants authorities turning a blind eye toward the depredations of rampaging youths such as those in Rocksprings. The Supreme Court of California's words are striking: "Often the public interest in tranquillity, security and protection is invoked only to be blithely dismissed, subordinated to the paramount right of the individual. In this case, however, the true nature of the tradeoff becomes painfully obvious. Liberty unrestrained is an invitation to anarchy. Freedom and responsibility are joined at the hip. 'Wise accommodation between liberty and order always has been and ever will be indispensable for a democratic society.'"

Catherine Coles and George Kelling, *Insight*, June 2, 1997.

The U.S. Supreme Court has repeatedly rejected such an interpretation, however, maintaining that the Constitution does not create a right to associate for social purposes. Only association that is directly linked to expressive purposes such as petitioning the government is constitutionally protected. In *The City of Dallas v. Stanglin*, for instance, the high court ruled against a dance hall owner who claimed that restricting 14- to 18-year-olds from his club late at night violated their associational rights. Furthermore, in *Bailey v. City of National City*, the court upheld a police department policy that caused an officer to be fired for his "continuous associations" with a known felon. The ruling was based on the grounds that, absent some significant expressive component, laws regulating social relationships are not subject to First Amendment scrutiny. In other words, for constitutional purposes, gang membership is not the equivalent of joining the National Association for the Advancement of Colored People (NAACP) or the Republican Party.

This is not to deny the fact that these injunctions can walk fine constitutional lines at times. Some judges have prohibited wearing gang insignia and displaying gang signs. While the First Amendment extends to all, "fighting words" have never been protected. The California high court should thus permit civil orders in this area when a trial court judge finds that, as a matter of fact, colors and signs are used to intimidate others in the community.

In an era of mandatory minimum sentences and high incarceration rates, civil injunctions provide a viable alternative to criminal convictions—a way for the community to intervene in wayward kids' lives before the trouble gets too serious. Moreover, by making it difficult for gangs to operate, injunctions make it harder for gangs to recruit impressionable youngsters in the first place. The ruling in *Acuna* has left Rocksprings residents afraid that they will be forced once again to keep their children indoors at all times, to return home themselves before dark, and to face violent retaliation for cooperating with police. It is the right of these citizens to the peaceful enjoyment of their homes and streets that deserves protection, and not some ersatz right to operate an intimidating gang.

"Rather than having oppressive ordinances, it would be more productive to discuss the factors that result in young people joining gangs."

GANG-LOITERING ORDINANCES ARE AN OBJECTIONABLE APPROACH TO REDUCING TEENAGE VIOLENCE

George Brooks

Ordinances that prohibit young people from gathering in public places are reprehensible, argues George Brooks in the following viewpoint. Brooks maintains that these laws are unjust and discriminatory because they target minorities and allow them to be arrested without any evidence of wrongdoing. Instead of condemning gang members, he contends, society needs to understand why youths join gangs and how to intervene in ways that will reduce youth violence. Brooks is the director of advocacy at Kolbe House, the jail ministry of the Archdiocese of Chicago, and a chaplain at Chicago's Cook County Jail.

As you read, consider the following questions:

1. What moral problems are created by gang-loitering ordinances, in the author's view?
2. According to Brooks, what is the responsibility of Christians toward young people who lack family support?
3. How do the U.S. Catholic bishops criticize the criminal-justice system, according to the author?

Reprinted from George Brooks, "Let's Not Gang Up on Our Kids," U.S. Catholic, March 1997, by permission of U.S. Catholic, published by Claretian Publications, 205 W. Monroe St., Chicago, IL 60606.

L aws based on stereotyping and guilt by association are being passed in the name of crime prevention. Laws that seemed impossible after the McCarthy era now encourage discriminatory and arbitrary law enforcement. Many of these laws are being found unconstitutional. All these laws are morally reprehensible.

OFFENSIVE ORDINANCES

In 1992, a Chicago ordinance provided that "whenever a police officer observes a person whom he reasonably believes to be a criminal street-gang member loitering in any public place with one or more other persons, he shall order such persons to disperse from the area." Failure of the suspect to not promptly obey would authorize his or her arrest. When the Illinois Appellate Court declared the law unconstitutional in 1995, many who saw the ordinance as a valid way to curb gang activity protested loudly. The court's decision was based on the ordinance's failure to include some type of illegal conduct besides loitering. In 1989 an ordinance was upheld in Milwaukee that prohibits "loitering in a place, at a time, or in a manner not used for law-abiding individuals." And in Tacoma, Washington, in 1992, an ordinance was upheld that prohibits loitering "in a manner and under circumstances manifesting the purpose to engage in drug-related activities."

Having my own law firm for 25 years, I find these ordinances legally objectionable. Yet these laws offend and outrage me even more because of my experiences over the past six years as a chaplain at Cook County Jail in Chicago. There I see young people confined for committing no crime other than being in a group. Many are guilty only by association or guilty because they adorned gang colors or gang insignias. Often the gang-loitering ordinance permits young people to be arrested for not doing anything illegal.

There are significant moral problems raised by gang-loitering ordinances. It is troubling when anyone can be singled out because of who they are with or the colors or symbols they are wearing rather than for what they are doing. If the ordinance were applied equally in all communities, regardless of race, ethnicity or social status, the country on the whole would be outraged. Rather than having oppressive ordinances, it would be more productive to discuss the factors that result in young people joining gangs and those conditions that can prevent them from becoming lawbreakers.

As a chaplain, I visit 72 inmates in 12 cellblocks every week as they wait for trial anywhere from a year to three years. The majority of the detainees are gang members, and most are black or Latino. Almost all of them live in poor neighborhoods.

This experience has made me more aware that the criminal-justice system works differently for them. My white, middle-class background did not prepare me for the systemic abuses that are routine for certain members of our society. The abuses start at the time of arrest, continue through bail setting, include plea bargaining, and end up in the sentencing. I hear story after story of young blacks and Latinos being stopped by the police, hassled, verbally abused, and searched.

They are stopped because of their race or ethnicity—not because of doing anything illegal. The presumption of innocence is virtually nonexistent. The poor are unable to post bond, so they remain incarcerated until their overworked public defender can get to their case. This only increases their antagonism for the police and reinforces the belief that it is "us" against the system. The arrest of innocent people can lead to their erroneous convictions. Since 1996, six minorities in Illinois alone have been released from death row in two separate cases because of evidence that absolved them from committing any crime.

Frequently I hear, "Well, if they're not doing anything wrong, why should they care if they get stopped and searched?" That's a nice sound bite, but I don't think many middle-class parents would tolerate their kids being stopped, insulted, and searched on a regular basis.

Recently three Latino young men came out to my home in the suburbs to pick up a couch and some clothes. Their van broke down on the expressway. Rather than getting assistance from the police, the young men and all the contents of the van were searched. They had to walk a mile to call for help. While I was angry about what happened, they were not upset. They expected blatant discriminatory practices; they didn't look at the police as those who would help them but as those who would hassle them.

THE REASONS FOR GANG MEMBERSHIP

In February 1995, the Chicago Crime Commission issued a report saying there were 100,000 gang members in the city. These figures indicate that 10 percent of Chicagoans between the ages of 9 and 40 are gang members. Although I question the methodology for arriving at these figures, the real question is: Are we just going to condemn gang members and lock them up as soon as possible or do we want to do something about the conditions that foster gang membership?

We must understand that young people join gangs for the family they don't have. They join for acceptance and security. They join because they don't have an education or job skills— gangs are how they can survive. Society can urge abrogating gang members' constitutional rights and demand they need family values, but isn't our Christian responsibility to help these kids? Our responsibility when good parents and a good family do not exist is to provide early and continuing intervention in young people's lives.

A Superficial Solution

Injunctions ignore the reality that gang activity is widespread as a result of critical, broad problems that permeate our society. Without addressing deficits in education, job opportunity, recreational resources and—most important—the breakdown of the family, superficial remedies like injunctions will be as effective as treating a heart attack with rubbing alcohol.

Allan Parachini, *Los Angeles Times*, February 23, 1997.

In 1996 Chicago went through a tragic trial of a juvenile. An 11-year-old male, with 28 prior arrests, was suspected of killing an innocent, talented 14-year-old girl. His gang then ordered his murder, which was carried out by 14- and 16-year-olds. Having been sexually abused as a youth and born to a teenage mother and a father who is now in prison, the 11-year-old was a felon at age 9. Early and continuing intervention may have made a difference.

Improving the Conditions

We need to be serious about youth crime. But we can't be serious when each kid does not have a decent and competitive education, a decent place to live, and decent health care. Each Christian has to be involved in changing detrimental conditions. Basic education, job training, conflict resolution, child-care skills, emotional support, substance abuse counseling, and meaningful jobs are all necessary. We can't ignore and lock up a child when those things do not exist.

Why not just immediately lock up the 100,000 gang members? Maybe because from a practical standpoint there aren't enough jail facilities. Or could it be that confining our youth is a violent solution?

In a 1995 letter "Confronting the Culture of Violence," the U.S. Catholic bishops wrote: "We are tragically turning to violence in search of the quick and easy answers to complex human problems. . . . How do we teach the young to curb their violence when we embrace it as the solution to social problems?" The bishops added that our criminal-justice system "does not offer security to society, just penalties and rehabilitation to offenders, or respect and restitution to victims." And they are right.

I first met Keith when he was 20 years old, a ten-year gang member. He dropped out of school when he was in fifth grade. He was arrested on a regular basis, frequently for just hanging out. He saw the police and courts as the enemy. He was usually released within a day or so with nothing being done to change his behavior or improve his life. But in jail, he responded to the influence of chaplains and quit the gang.

In court, Keith was found not guilty by a jury, not on any technicality, but because he hadn't committed any crime. (Keith and two other former gang members were arrested without any evidence of their involvement in a crime.) Today Keith has a job as a mentor for a social service agency and is going to school.

Keith is an example of why we need to build fewer prisons and rebuild more lives. We need to confine fewer young people and do more freeing of spirits and souls. We need to commit fewer people to institutions and commit to all people. It will only be when each member of our faith community takes responsibility to live the gospel that our society will refocus its priorities for the dignity and respect of each person.

| "When boot camps are used as an alternative to confinement, savings can be achieved."

JUVENILE BOOT CAMPS CAN BE EFFECTIVE IN ADDRESSING TEENAGE CRIME

Eric Peterson

In the following viewpoint, Eric Peterson contends that boot camps for juvenile criminals, which provide military-style discipline and physical training, can have positive results. He asserts that participants' academic skills improve and that many of these youths find jobs after leaving the camp. In addition, he claims, boot camps are less costly than traditional confinement. While Peterson concedes that these programs are not as successful as more traditional programs at reducing recidivism, he argues that boot camps can achieve their goals if they follow certain guidelines. Peterson is a program manager in the Office of Juvenile Justice and Delinquency Prevention's (OJJDP) Research and Program Development Division.

As you read, consider the following questions:

1. According to Peterson, what was the program completion rate in Cleveland?
2. In the author's view, what population should be targeted for boot camp?
3. What services should aftercare programs provide, according to Peterson?

Reprinted from Eric Peterson, "Juvenile Boot Camps: Lessons Learned," at www.ncjrs.org/txtfiles/fs-9636.txt, cited December 21, 1997.

In response to a significant increase in juvenile arrests and re- peat offenses over the past decade, several States and many lo- calities have established juvenile boot camps. The first juvenile boot camp programs, modeled after boot camps for adult of- fenders, emphasized military-style discipline and physical con- ditioning. The Office of Juvenile Justice and Delinquency Preven- tion (OJJDP) has supported the development of three juvenile boot camp demonstration sites. This viewpoint describes those demonstration projects, their evaluations, and lessons learned that will benefit future boot camp programs.

HIGHLY STRUCTURED PROGRAMS

In 1992 OJJDP funded three juvenile boot camps designed to address the special needs and circumstances of adolescent of- fenders. The programs were conducted in Cleveland, Ohio; Den- ver, Colorado; and Mobile, Alabama.

Focusing on a target population of adjudicated, nonviolent offenders under the age of 18, the boot camp programs were designed as highly structured, 3-month residential programs followed by 6 to 9 months of community-based aftercare. Dur- ing the aftercare period, youth were to pursue academic and vo- cational training or employment while under intensive, but pro- gressively diminishing, supervision.

OJJDP undertook impact evaluations for all three sites that compared the recidivism rates for juveniles who participated in the pilot programs with those of control groups. The evaluations also compared the cost-effectiveness of juvenile boot camps with other dispositional alternatives. Reports of the three impact evaluations are available. The evaluations of the Mobile and Cleveland programs are interim reports that present data from the earliest cohorts. As neither program had stabilized when the data were collected, OJJDP is considering expanding the evalua- tion to include the remaining cohorts. The Denver program is no longer active.

SUCCESS AND FAILURE

Most juvenile boot camp participants completed the residential program and graduated to aftercare. Program completion rates were 96 percent in Cleveland, 87 percent in Mobile, and 76 per- cent in Denver.

At the two sites where educational gains were measured, sub- stantial improvements in academic skills were noted. In Mobile approximately three-quarters of the participants improved their performance in reading, spelling, language, and math by one grade level or more. In Cleveland the average juvenile boot camp participant improved reading, spelling, and math skills by approximately one grade level.

In addition, where employment records were available, a significant number of participants found jobs while in aftercare.

The pilot programs, however, did not demonstrate a reduction in recidivism. In Denver and Mobile, no statistically significant difference could be found between the recidivism rates of juvenile boot camp participants and those of the control groups (youth confined in State or county institutions, or released on probation). In Cleveland pilot program participants evidenced a higher recidivism rate than juvenile offenders confined in traditional juvenile correctional facilities. It should be noted that none of the sites fully implemented OJJDP's model juvenile boot camp guidelines, and that some critical aftercare support services were not provided.

LESSONS LEARNED

Several significant lessons have emerged from the pilot programs:

The appropriate population should be targeted. Boot camps should be designed as an intermediate intervention. At one site, youth who had been previously confined were significantly more likely to recidivate, while youth with the least serious offenses were also more likely to recidivate.

Facility location is important. Cost issues and community resistance were major obstacles to securing residential and aftercare facilities. To increase attendance and reduce problems, aftercare facilities should be located in gang-neutral areas accessible by public transportation.

Staff selection and training needs are critical. To reduce staff turnover, fill gaps in critical services, and ensure consistent programming, the screening, selection, and training of juvenile boot camp and aftercare staff must be sensitive to the programmatic and operational features of a juvenile boot camp. This is particularly important with regard to youth development issues.

THE IMPORTANCE OF AFTERCARE

Moreover, continuous treatment between the residential and aftercare phases should be integrated philosophically and programmatically, particularly through staffing.

Aftercare programs are challenging to implement. Successful aftercare programs require attention at the outset to develop a comprehensive model with the flexibility to respond to local needs and concerns. Aftercare programs are unlikely to succeed if their participants fail to receive the full range of services prescribed for them. Aftercare programs must be broad-based and flexible enough to meet the particular educational, employment, counseling, and support needs of each participant. The aftercare component should form dynamic linkages with other community services, especially youth service agencies, schools, and employers.

Results from a Florida Boot Camp

Some statistics from a Department of Juvenile Justice study of the first five platoons in 1994 and 1995 to go through the Leon County, Florida, Boot Camp:

- Typical age of a boot camp graduate: 16

- Average number of court cases before admission to camp: 11.3

- 46 percent of graduates were committed for felony property offenses; 30 percent for felonies against persons; 10 percent for drug felony crimes.

- As a group, boot camp graduates increased approximately one grade level in reading; one grade and three months in both math and language.

- 43 percent of graduates were employed after release from boot camp, most in fast-food chains and retail and grocery stores.

- 71 percent of the graduates were re-arrested within one year of graduation, a slightly lower rate than a comparable group of non-camp juvenile offenders, whose rate was 75 percent.

Chris Poynter, *Tallahassee (Fla.) Democrat*, February 23, 1997.

Coordination among agencies must be maintained. All three sites experienced difficulties in maintaining coordination among the participating agencies. Considerable attention should be paid to building and maintaining a consensus among participating organizations concerning the program's philosophy and procedures.

Evaluating the Results

Effective evaluation begins with planning. To assess the program's successes and failures, quantifiable data should be collected about participation in treatment by juveniles in the boot camp and in the control group. Measures of program success should include a broad spectrum of outcomes. Recidivism measures should capture all subsequent delinquent activity, not simply the first new adjudication, and data on new offenses should include information on the origin and circumstances of the complaint to determine whether there is a monitoring effect, in which the intensity of the supervision causes an increase in recorded offending.

When boot camps are used as an alternative to confinement, savings can be achieved. Communities often implement juvenile boot camps, in part, to reduce costs. The experience of the pilot sites indicates that when boot camps are used as an alternative to traditional confinement, costs can be reduced considerably because of the significantly shorter residential stay. However, if boot camps are used as an alternative to probation, savings will not be realized.

Juvenile boot camps embrace a variety of objectives: reducing recidivism, improving academic performance, cutting the cost of treating juvenile offenders, and inculcating the values of self-discipline and hard work. In attempting to reach these objectives, OJJDP is collaborating with the Office of Justice Programs (OJP) to enhance program models, policies, and practices of juvenile boot camps. As a result, many of the lessons learned from OJJDP's three demonstration sites have been incorporated in the OJP Boot Camp Corrections Program.

| "Juvenile boot camps will neither reduce crime nor save on prison costs."

JUVENILE BOOT CAMPS DO NOT REDUCE TEENAGE CRIME

Margaret Beyer

In the following viewpoint, Margaret Beyer argues that military-style boot camps for young offenders will not reduce juvenile crime. These camps are ineffective because they fail to provide nurturing or promote independence, Beyer contends. In addition, she asserts, boot camps ignore teenagers' desire for fairness and their resistance to imposed structure. Beyer claims that approaches to juvenile crime that focus on empowering and encouraging youths are preferable to boot camps. Beyer is a psychologist based in Washington, D.C., who works with juvenile delinquents and their families.

As you read, consider the following questions:

1. What are Paul DeMuro's criticisms of boot camps, as cited by Beyer?
2. According to the author, what is the recidivism rate of the boot camps in Florida and Ohio?
3. Why is young people's rejection of unfair and punitive adults a strength, in Beyer's view?

Reprinted from Margaret Beyer, "Juvenile Boot Camps Don't Make Sense," *Criminal Justice*, Fall 1995; ©1995 American Bar Association. Reprinted with permission.

A lthough juvenile crime is not on the rise, the public, misinformed by politicians and the press, insists on increasingly cruel methods to punish young offenders.

There are more adolescents in the population so there are more juvenile arrests, but this does not justify giving up on rehabilitative approaches. Overall juvenile crime has been decreasing since 1992. Based on 1992 data, the Department of Justice (DOJ) acknowledged that juveniles are not responsible for most of the increase in violent crime. "If juvenile violence had not increased between 1988 and 1992, the U.S. violent crime rate would have increased 16 percent instead of 23 percent." In fact, the arrest rate for juveniles actually dropped slightly between 1991 and 1993: 16,036 per 100,000 were arrested in 1989, 16,893 per 100,000 were arrested in 1991, and 16,681 per 100,000 were arrested in 1993. Juvenile arrest rates for property offenses decreased while juvenile arrest rates for violent offenses increased between 1989 and 1993.

BOOT CAMPS DO NOT SAVE MONEY

Since 1980, younger and younger teenagers have been treated as adult criminals. Boot camps for juveniles are the latest in this dangerous trend and will be as ineffective as wholesale incarceration of youth in adult facilities. Yet the message has not gotten out to state legislatures and corrections departments that juvenile boot camps will neither reduce crime nor save on prison costs.

There have been surprisingly few voices against juvenile boot camps. Paul DeMuro, an independent consultant in Montclair, New Jersey, wrote the 1995 unpublished report on juvenile boot camps, "Where Do We Go from Here?" for the Annie E. Casey Foundation. DeMuro has drawn attention to deaths in boot camps, the use of military discipline to disguise staff mistreatment particularly of minority youth, and the absence of followup supports when youth return to their communities. He has predicted an increase in adult court referrals as youth who fail to complete boot camps or are rearrested after their release are no longer viewed as eligible for juvenile court. Dale Parent, a senior analyst at ABT Associates in Massachusetts, demonstrates through statistical analysis that juvenile boot camps cannot save money unless they have hundreds of beds and the stay is limited to three months—conditions all agree would make the programs pointless. His report, "Planning a Boot Camp," was written for the Department of Justice, Office of Justice Programs Boot Camp Technical Assistance Workshop, held April 1, 1995. Furthermore, Parent emphasizes that juvenile boot camps are widening the net by including youth who previously would not have been locked up—boot camps could only reduce correctional costs if participants are selected from the population already qualified for incarceration. David Altschuler, a professor and researcher at Johns Hopkins Institute for Policy Studies, is directing a long-term study of aftercare for juveniles leaving secure facilities. The study is funded by the DOJ's Office of Juvenile Justice and Delinquency Prevention (OJJDP). Altschuler has argued that incarceration is only as effective as the reintegration services supporting youths to avoid their former criminal lifestyle when they return home. He points out that juvenile boot camps are limited to "shock incarceration" and keep costs down by leaving aftercare to overloaded probation and parole officers. Without any documentation that boot camps decrease delinquency—and, in fact, reports that two early juvenile boot camps (in Florida and Ohio) had recidivism rates of 70 percent—millions of federal and state dollars are going into juvenile boot camp construction and operation.

THE REASONS BOOT CAMPS FAIL

Since the observations of prominent juvenile justice experts and the absence of positive outcome studies have not deterred incarceration-minded politicians, perhaps we should consider educating the public about the dangers of juvenile boot camps through their experiences as parents. Parents search for a wise balance of love and limits to meet their teenagers' needs. The adult criminal system in general, and boot camps in particular, fail the basic test of balancing nurturing and opportunities for independence. Everyone who has been the parent of a teenager knows that boot camps cannot be effective because they violate the basic principles of adolescent development:

• *Teenagers are fairness fanatics:* Operating successful group programs for this age group is difficult because most adolescents are moralistic and intolerant of anything that seems unfair. They especially see group punishment as unfair.

• *Teenagers reject imposed structure:* Although they benefit from limits, adolescents object to being forced to adhere to structure in which they did not have a voice. "Authority problems" in schools and correctional programs can be, at least in part, attributed to insistence on controlling youth who are accustomed to running their own lives. Many youth who have been physically or sexually abused or exposed to substance abuse or domestic violence in their families react especially negatively to imposed outside controls.

• *Teenagers respond to encouragement:* Although youth may alter their behavior momentarily to avoid adverse consequences, attitudes and behaviors seldom change as a result of punishment.

BOOT CAMPS ARE NOT CONSIDERED EFFECTIVE

In 1995, the National League of Cities (NLC) published its annual survey of municipal officials. "Assuring public safety" was among the three highest priorities of the 383 elected municipal officials (drawn from a random sample in cities with populations of 10,000 or more) who responded to the survey. . . .

The most preferred policy—"strengthening and supporting family stability, selected by 64 percent—reflects a growing sentiment that public safety needs to be considered in a much broader context than traditional anti-crime solutions."

The policies and programs believed by municipal officials in the NLC survey as most likely to reduce crime are:

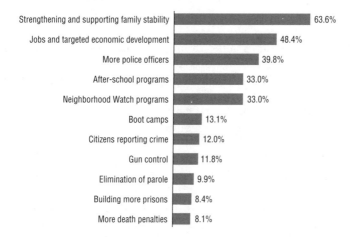

Strengthening and supporting family stability	63.6%
Jobs and targeted economic development	48.4%
More police officers	39.8%
After-school programs	33.0%
Neighborhood Watch programs	33.0%
Boot camps	13.1%
Citizens reporting crime	12.0%
Gun control	11.8%
Elimination of parole	9.9%
Building more prisons	8.4%
More death penalties	8.1%

Richard A. Mendel, *Prevention or Pork? A Hard-Headed Look at Youth-Oriented Anti-Crime Programs*, 1995.

Given their reaction against unfairness, imposed structure, and punishment, it is not surprising that young people reject what might be offered as assistance when they mistrust the adults in charge as unfair, controlling, and punitive. This rejection of "help" is a strength—it is the way that young people have survived the adversity of poverty and racism. If this mistrust of unfair, controlling, and punitive adults is subdued, it undermines the very survival technique that has allowed these youths to make it as far as they have.

PROGRAMS THAT WORK

Ironically, as states build juvenile boot camps that are likely to fail, the ingredients for services that enable delinquents to invest in noncriminal futures are well-known. Delinquents change their behavior when services build on their strengths and meet their needs. Programs such as Associated Marine Institutes in Florida and other states, Youth Advocacy Program in Pennsylvania, Children's Trust Neighborhood Initiative in Washington, D.C., Alternative Rehabilitative Communities (ARC) in Pennsylvania, Kaleidoscope in Illinois, and the family treatment program at the Medical University of South Carolina have high success rates with delinquents. These programs have several characteristics in common:

• *They meet each youth's need to feel competent at something.* These programs provide opportunities for success and celebrate each youth's competence. Recognizing that school and noncriminal employment have been inaccessible, these programs offer youths real preparation for self-respecting work.

• *They meet each youth's need to be in charge.* These programs emphasize making choices and encourage genuine youth involvement in designing the daily routine and carrying out tasks.

• *They meet each youth's need to appreciate the strengths of their families.* These programs empower families and support young people in identifying with the positive characteristics of family members and making peace with the disappointments and hurt from their families.

• *They meet each youth's need to belong.* These programs offer a nonviolent group as desirable as a gang that gives recognition and encouragement and is hopeful about the future.

Programs that are effective with serious juvenile offenders recognize that if the young people do not want what we think they need, little will change in their lives. However well meaning the staff, young people will react against the imposed structure, punishment, and unfairness of juvenile boot camps. Even when they have committed serious crimes, young people have different needs than adults.

> "[Kids] settle disagreements or conflicts violently because they haven't been taught to do it non-violently."

PEACE EDUCATION CAN HELP REDUCE TEENAGE VIOLENCE

Colman McCarthy

Courses in peace education can reduce violence in schools, asserts Colman McCarthy in the following viewpoint. He maintains that youths are not naturally wild but that they use violence to solve conflicts because they have not been taught nonviolent methods. Learning nonviolent conflict resolution is just as important as learning math and science, McCarthy contends. He also claims that society's attitudes and responses toward violence need to change in order for peace education to succeed. McCarthy is a syndicated columnist.

As you read, consider the following questions:

1. Why did Walter Annenberg focus on youth violence, as quoted by the author?
2. According to McCarthy, how many of the high school students he spoke to learned peacemaking in grade school?
3. What measures directed toward reducing youth violence does McCarthy criticize?

Reprinted, with permission, from Colman McCarthy, "Peace Education," *Liberal Opinion Week*, January 3, 1994; ©1994, The Washington Post Writers Group.

In Walter Annenberg's statements accompanying his $500 million gift to help reform public education, the philanthropist focused on one issue: youthful violence. Unless countered, he said at a White House ceremony, it "will not only erode the educational system but will destroy our way of life." To halt "this tragedy" of violence, "education is the most wholesome and effective approach."

Annenberg has been heeding some enlightened advisers. To decrease violence by and among the young, he has directed his generous sum—the largest gift ever to public education—to classroom reforms, not metal detectors, hallway cops, playground police or prisons. A sizable portion of the $500 million is to be devoted to curriculum improvement. Agonizing searches aren't needed on where best to begin: the creation or expansion of academically rigorous courses on non-violent conflict resolution, mediation and peace studies.

IGNORANCE LEADS TO VIOLENCE

Kids aren't shooting or beating each other, or their teachers, because they're inherently unruly but because they're academically uninformed. They settle disagreements or conflicts violently because they haven't been taught to do it non-violently. Ignorance, not evil, is the problem.

When speaking before college audiences, I ask students for a show of hands on two questions. How many attended a high school that offered courses on conflict resolution? Rarely is a hand raised. Question two: How many went to a high school where courses on math and science were taught? Every hand goes up.

It's the same at high school assemblies: How many went to a grade school that taught courses in peacemaking? None. And math and science courses? All.

If it's considered useful for children to know about trapezoids and nitric oxide—knowledge that may or may not be relevant in their adulthoods—then why not educate them in the art of non-violent conflict resolution, which they'll always need? They'll be having conflicts all their lives—at home, the workplace and most points between—and the solutions to them will be either violent or non-violent.

SOCIETY TEACHES VIOLENCE

Even if taught non-violence, children are saturated by lessons in violence by other teachers beyond the classrooms: fathers or mothers who may be physically or emotionally abusive at home, actors who prostitute their talents in gun movies, fistfighting athletes in football, hockey and baseball games, presidents who send troops to bomb people in Third World conflicts, politicians and attorneys general who back the death penalty, pro-choicers who champion the killing of fetal life as a right, military contractors whose arms dealing has made the United States the world's leading weapons seller, hunters who take pleasure in killing animals.

A Successful Mediation Program

Some school-based prevention programs are centered around mediation. In such programs, students are trained by teachers to be mediators who work with their fellow students in negotiating the settlement of disputes. One such program is the Resolving Conflict Creatively Program (RCCP), which seeks to create a climate of nonviolence in schools. The program started in New York in 1985 and can be found in the Anchorage school districts (Alaska), the New Orleans public schools (Louisiana), the South-Orange Maplewood School District (New Jersey), and the Vista United school districts (California). The program stresses the need for nonviolent alternatives for dealing with conflict, negotiation, and other conflict resolution skills. The lessons involve role playing, interviewing, group dialogue, brainstorming, and other experiential learning techniques. An important aspect of the program is parent training through a Parent Involvement Program component. This consists of a team of two or three parents per school, who are trained for sixty hours in family communication and conflict resolution.

Evaluation of the program indicates that teachers are enthusiastic about the program, and they report decreased levels of violence among the students in the program. Students in the program report that they are now able to resolve their conflict without violence, and they have fewer fights and name-calling.

Janice Joseph, *Black Youths, Delinquency, and Juvenile Justice,* 1995.

Against that onslaught—much of it legal, socially acceptable or politically popular—schools that might be given Annenberg money to put peace education into the curriculum will be bucking stiff headwinds. But what other choice is present? Give up? Hope the Brady bill does it?

If the current pattern holds, kids in school today—from first grade to 12th grade—will be dealing with their conflicts in a few years, or sooner, by swinging their fists or shooting their guns. Then Congress will pass another crime bill with billions for new prisons, the Department of Education will issue another study on school violence, church leaders will call for prayer days and the networks will carry specials on kids who attacked their teachers.

THERE ARE SOLUTIONS

At the White House ceremony with Walter Annenberg, President Bill Clinton said, "Nearly every problem has been solved somewhere by somebody." On school violence, he's right. Such proven peace educators as Fran Schmidt in Miami, Neil Katz in Syracuse, Timothy Shriver in New Haven, Michael Nagler in California, Ian Harris in Milwaukee and many others have been in classrooms teaching both the techniques of non-violence and the literature of peacemaking.

Solutions to violence exist and can be studied, absorbed and practiced in the nation's 28,000 high schools and 78,000 grade schools. How much of the Annenberg gift eventually goes to peace education will tell whether this is a serious or cosmetic reform.

"Hundreds of grassroots leaders . . . have shown how the same mechanisms that are a conduit for drugs and crime can be used to import productive, healing activities."

COMMUNITY-BASED EFFORTS CAN HELP REDUCE TEENAGE VIOLENCE

Robert L. Woodson Sr.

In the following viewpoint, Robert L. Woodson Sr. argues that community-based programs are more effective than national strategies in solving youth violence. Woodson contends that the people who lead these grassroots efforts earn the trust and respect of young people and show youths how to serve their families and communities. Strategies that focus on incarceration backfire, he maintains, because prisons actually breed further violence. Woodson is the president and founder of the Washington, D.C.-based National Center for Neighborhood Enterprise.

As you read, consider the following questions:
1. According to Woodson, what are "wolf pack" attacks?
2. How many Americans are in gangs, according to the author?
3. What is the "bridge program," as described by Woodson?

Reprinted from Robert L. Woodson Sr., "National Youth Gang Strategy Inadequate," *Headway*, December 1996, by permission of *Headway*.

During the summer of 1983, the city of Philadelphia was paralyzed with fear as small gangs of marauding black youths arbitrarily targeted citizens on the streets and in shopping malls. In what police termed as "wolf pack" attacks, the victims were knocked to the ground and stripped of rings, watches, gold chains, wallets and purses. A virtual reign of terror spread as reports of the attacks were published and other youths joined in the melee.

A Solution in Philadelphia

Because these robberies were not connected to organized gangs and occurred sporadically, police and law enforcement officials found it impossible to predict or contain the rash of attacks. Neither increased police patrols or emergency funding to traditional social service institutions had any impact on the problem.

As the City was held hostage in this crime wave, movie theaters closed early, stores and shopping centers shut down, and many civic events were canceled. Public officials were at a point of hopelessness when two grassroots leaders stepped forward and suggested a unique strategy. Within one day of the implementation of their plan, the attacks ceased and never again resumed.

The identities of these leaders and how they accomplished this feat contain valuable lessons for addressing a current epidemic of youth crime and gang violence. David and Falaka Fattah were well-known veteran black activists who had discovered that one of their own six sons was an active gang member. At that time, Philadelphia was known as the youth gang capital of the nation. Newspapers published weekly gang violence victim statistics next to the death tolls of the Vietnam War.

In responding to their son's gang activity, the Fattahs reached out to embrace his circle of friends rather than trying to isolate him from them, inviting 13 of the youths to come to live with them in their small row house in West Philadelphia. This informal arrangement blossomed into a gang rescue program called the House of Umoja.

Creating a Peace Pact

Word of the safe-haven soon spread on the streets and the number of young gang members seeking asylum steadily increased. Within a few years, the influence of the Fattah's outreach spread throughout the entire city, and they were able to coordinate a city-wide peace pact that dramatically reduced the annual number of gang-related homicides.

The Fattahs brought this established reputation and foundation of trust and respect with them when they came to the table to address the crisis of the wolf-pack attacks. Their first step was to call in the "experts" with invaluable street experience, former gang members—the "Old Heads" or "Ogs"—they had worked with. This group suggested a collaborative effort with their counterparts who were incarcerated at the local prison, "the House of Correction."

When the call went out for help in stopping the violence, more than 130 inmates signed up to join a crime-prevention task force. The prisoners identified young people who were influential on their "corners" in their neighborhoods who were invited to a conference at the prison the following Saturday.

The response was overwhelming. On the day of the conference, buses ferried more than 300 youths to the prison. After hearing presentations from the inmates on personal responsibility and moral obligation, the group broke up into smaller work shops and discussion groups focused on ending the violence. The following day peace prevailed.

A LACK OF SUPPORT

Although the Fattahs and their group received official recognition from the mayor, the acknowledgement of their unique ability to reach the city's young people was more ceremonial than substantive. When funds were later allocated for crime prevention or youth services, they were designated for conventional social service programs and for increased police patrols. The Fattahs were applauded but then ignored.

Our national strategy, likewise, has failed to provide substantial support for alternative grassroots responses to youth crime and gang activity, in spite of the undeniable effectiveness. While plaques may be bestowed on numerous successful neighborhood-based anti-gang efforts, there has been no effort to develop structures that can harness the capacities of grassroots initiatives in order to sustain and expand their impact. Instead, as in the case of the Fattahs, massive funding has been channeled to conventional social programs, therapeutic intervention, and police interdiction and incarceration.

One definition of insanity is to keep doing the same thing, but to expect different results. As budgets for conventional, failed programs have expanded, the crisis has continued to mount. We are now at a point where, in the words of Attorney General Janet Reno, "Gang violence has spread to every corner of America."

A nationwide survey has reported that gang membership in

the United States has grown to more than 650,000 members who are involved in 25,000 gangs. Youth crime is taking America hostage, one community, one industry at a time. Like the shopping plazas of Philadelphia, one internationally acclaimed mall in Minnesota has considered instituting a curfew because of an onslaught of gang fights.

PRISONS WORSEN VIOLENCE

In response, a massive crackdown was launched by the FBI, the Safe Streets Initiative, which created 133 task forces that resulted in 92,000 arrests and 35,000 convictions nationwide throughout a four-year period. Yet, in the words of one corrections director in Illinois—a state where half of the 38,000 prison population has been identified as gang members—"The problem does not go away. When the community gets rid of its gang problem that problem is then transferred to the correctional institution. In fact, it becomes more intensified."

No more Excuses

Two excuses I've grown particularly weary of hearing over the years are these: (1) there's no guarantee that your efforts will result in saving a kid, and (2) you can't save everybody. As general statements, both of those are undeniably true; as excuses, both of them are shamefully lame. Of course there are no guarantees. But we can guarantee what will happen if we *don't* get involved. Kids will keep selling crack to mothers. They will keep screwing up their own lives and those of their friends and relatives. They will keep terrorizing the neighborhoods. They will keep killing each other. Guaran-damn-teed. And of course you can't save everybody. But why should that prevent you from saving *somebody*? . . .

There are no more excuses if you genuinely want the homies to live, because now you know. You might not know about budgets and buildings and meeting agendas but you know that you have to be there for the kids; that you have to help them deal with their anger, fear, and pain; that you have to provide them with the knowledge they need to recognize and steer clear of risky behavior; that you have to give them positive rules for living.

Joseph Marshall Jr. and Lonnie Wheeler, *Street Soldier: One Man's Struggle to Save a Generation—One Life at a Time*, 1996.

In short, rising rates of incarceration of youthful offenders have turned our prisons into breeding grounds of violence and mayhem, which are now being exported back again into the community. Shocking evidence has emerged of gang recruitment and the formation of inter-gang alliances even within prison walls, and chains of command from the prisons to the streets remain undisturbed.

In Washington, D.C., for example, an investigation revealed that Rayful Edmonds, the head of a notorious drug ring who is currently serving a life sentence, has been coordinating a drug trafficking operation from his prison cell which is far more expansive and lucrative than the dynasty he ruled when he was on the outside. From Connecticut to California, homicides have been traced to death orders issued by inmates.

In spite of the daunting scale of this crisis, remedies do exist—in a multitude of replications of the Philadelphia model. Throughout the country, hundreds of grassroots leaders, who have earned the trust and respect of thousands of people they have served, have shown how the same mechanisms that are a conduit for drugs and crime can be used to import productive, healing activities and life-transforming experiences.

SUCCESS STORIES

In Washington, D.C., a group of six ex-offenders formed the Alliance of Concerned Men, an organization dedicated to recognizing and utilizing the capacities of inmates and establishing links through which men who are incarcerated can continue—or begin—to serve their families and communities. As one of ACM's founders, Tyrone Parker explains, "We believe that a man does not relinquish his responsibilities upon incarceration."

Using strategies similar to the Fattahs', the Alliance established a "bridge program" which facilitates prison visits and communication between incarcerated men and their children, and a unique "Adopt-a-Block" program, through which groups of inmates use their influence on the streets to keep their neighborhoods violence free.

From coast to coast, similar efforts are underway, utilizing indigenous community networks and gang structures to constructive ends. In Los Angeles, Leon Watkins tirelessly worked with one young gang leader until he established the trust that led to his transformation. Working together, they then brought hundreds of other youths through that same threshold of opportunity.

In Hartford, Conn., through the investment of one man, Carl Hardrick, five former leaders of the city's most notorious gangs are now working daily to spread the message of peace, productive community service, and prospects for young entrepreneurs. This small group of neighborhood leaders with street names like "Big Bird," "Book," and "Chan," are responsible for dramatically reducing the level of street violence in their city.

The problems of gang violence and youth crime now threaten us as an "American Chernobyl" that is ready to explode. Remedies do exist, but if we are to substantiate the hope they offer, we must be willing to re-channel our investments in past failures to risk success with new strategies implemented by unconventional experts. A virtual army of healers is ready to be mobilized.

PERIODICAL BIBLIOGRAPHY

The following articles have been selected to supplement the diverse views presented in this chapter. Addresses are provided for periodicals not indexed in the *Readers' Guide to Periodical Literature*, the *Alternative Press Index*, the *Social Sciences Index*, or the *Index to Legal Periodicals and Books*.

Awake!	"Protecting Our Children from Gangs," April 22, 1998. Available from Watchtower Bible and Tract Society of New York, 25 Columbia Heights, Brooklyn, NY 11201-2483.
Christian Science Monitor	"Juvenile Justice: Trying to Break Cycle of Crime," July 29, 1996.
John J. DiIulio Jr. et al.	"Crime Solutions: 18 Things We Can Now Do to Fight Back," *American Enterprise*, May-June 1995.
Craig Donegan	"Preventing Juvenile Crime," *CQ Researcher*, March 15, 1996. Available from 1414 22nd St. NW, Washington, DC 20037.
Issues and Controversies On File	"Teen Curfews," August 30, 1996. Available from Facts On File News Service, 11 Penn Plaza, New York, NY 10001-2006.
Richard Lacayo	"Teen Crime," *Time*, July 21, 1997.
John Leo	"Punished for the Sins of the Children," *U.S. News & World Report*, June 12, 1995.
Paul J. McNulty	"Natural Born Killers? Preventing the Coming Explosion of Teenage Crime," *Policy Review*, Winter 1995.
Kurt S. Olsson	"The Juvenile Justice Dilemma," *Corrections Today*, February 1996.
Mary Ann Perga	"Parents Shouldn't Do the Time When Kids Do the Crime," *U.S. Catholic*, December 1996.
Nina Siegal	"Ganging Up on Civil Liberties," *Progressive*, October 1997.
Atom Clay Thompson	"Organizers," *Third Force*, March-April 1998.
Laurel Shaper Walters	"States to Parents: Pay for Your Children's Crimes," *Christian Science Monitor*, April 1, 1996.
Nancy Watzman	"The Curfew Revival Gains Momentum," *Governing*, February 1994.

CHAPTER 3

HOW CAN TEEN PREGNANCY BE PREVENTED?

Chapter Preface

In Idaho, a 1921 law remains on the books holding that unmarried people who have sex "shall be found guilty of fornication." The statute was essentially defunct until 1996, when Gem County, Idaho, resurrected it as a method to discourage teenage pregnancy. In applying the law, Gem County prosecutor Douglas Varie targets pregnant teenagers and their boyfriends. One such teenager, seventeen-year-old Amanda Smisek, was convicted and sentenced to three years of probation, plus parenting classes.

Among Varie's critics is the American Civil Liberties Union (ACLU). Jack Van Valkenburgh, executive director of the ACLU of Idaho, states, "To the extent that the prosecutions are targeting teenagers, and the law applies to everybody, it is selective prosecution, and it denies equal protection of the law." Moreover, warn opponents, while the law will not keep teenagers from having sex, the threat of arrest could prevent teens from seeking birth control. For this reason, some maintain that the enforcement of fornication laws will actually increase teenage pregnancy.

However, Gem County officials assert that prosecutorial discretion—a prosecutor's freedom to determine which cases to prosecute—allows Varie to apply the fornication law as he sees fit. Furthermore, those who support Varie's approach claim that aggressive measures are justified when it comes to teenage pregnancy. These critics contend that since children born out of wedlock are more likely to end up in prison, on drugs, poor, and illiterate, they place a significant burden on society. Varie argues that "the cost [to society] isn't just in welfare. A male child of a single teen mother is three times more likely to go to jail as a child with two parents." Due to the high social costs of teenage pregnancy, Varie and others maintain, prosecuting unmarried teens for having sex is necessary.

Gem County's revival of the fornication statute reflects a nationwide move toward combating teen pregnancy with legislation. In California, for example, adult males who impregnate teenage girls can be prosecuted under statutory rape laws, which prohibit sex between adults and minors. While some laud these measures as effective ways to deter teenage pregnancy, others contend that a punitive approach to teenage pregnancy fails to address its root causes. The following chapter provides diverse views on how teenage pregnancy can be prevented.

| "Parents exercise a powerful influence
over their teens' sexual behavior."

TEACHING ABSTINENCE HELPS AVERT TEEN PREGNANCY

Maggie Gallagher

Maggie Gallagher argues in the following viewpoint that encouraging teenagers to abstain from sex can help prevent teenage pregnancy. Furthermore, she asserts, parents have a great deal of influence over whether their teenagers remain virgins. Gallagher is a nationally syndicated columnist.

As you read, consider the following questions:

1. According to the study cited by Gallagher, what three factors help parents discourage their teens from having sex?
2. In the author's words, how likely are teenagers to remain virgins if their parents discourage them from having sex?
3. What is the single biggest influence on whether or not teens have sex in the author's opinion?

From Maggie Gallagher, "Straight Talk About Sex Education," The Washington Times, January 29, 1997. Reprinted by permission of Universal Press Syndicate. All rights reserved.

Whon responsible adults talk to teen-agers about sex, what should we say?

Sex education is now as American as apple pie. On the importance of honest and open sexual communication with kids, Americans are agreed. But what we don't quite know, in our heart of hearts, is just what we should communicate: Do we push abstinence, contraceptives or both?

Programs pushing abstinence only remain highly controversial in some places, the subject of lawsuits by groups like Planned Parenthood, which has argued that schools invade teens' privacy if they don't unroll condoms on bananas in classrooms.

MODERN-DAY SEXUAL VALUES

Teens having sex are now considered normal. It's the virgins who have to explain their peculiar behavior. Meanwhile, parents who don't have pillow talks about the pill with their teens (and don't want condoms handed out in schools) face what can only be called social stigma.

Dana Mack, author of the book *The Assault on Parenthood*, relates the experience of one parent who stood up at a school board meeting to voice her opposition to condom distribution: "It's parents like you that are the reason why we need these machines," a school board member sneered back.

In the face of the MTVing of America, parents with traditional sexual values are apt to feel quaint, if not overwhelmed and impotent. That's too bad. Because several surprising studies suggest that protecting your teens from premature sex is hardly an impossible dream.

One study published in the summer of 1996 in *Family Planning Perspectives*, for example, found that even after controlling for various psychosocial factors (including self-esteem), parents exercise a powerful influence over their teens' sexual behavior.

THREE FACTORS IN HELPING TEENS POSTPONE SEX

If parents want to help their teens postpone sex, this study found, three factors are important: (1) Maintain a good, warm relationship with your child (children are far more likely to accept family values if they feel valued by their family). (2) Let your teens know openly and honestly you expect them not to have sex. And (3) avoid discussing birth control.

Separately each factor about doubles the likelihood that a teen will choose to postpone sex. Put them together, and the power of parents multiplies: A teen who has all three things going for him—warm parents who push abstinence and who don't push contraception—is *twelve-and-a-half times* more likely to remain a virgin than a teen who has none of these things.

And this is not only true of white middle-class families. This study investigated 751 African-American teens and their mothers in Philadelphia, proving that strong moms can protect their kids, even in places, such as urban black neighborhoods, that too many Middle Americans write off.

Parents Can Make a Difference

"I think one important message is that parents can make a difference," the study's principal author, James Jaccard, a psychology professor at SUNY-Albany, told the *Philadelphia Inquirer.* "Many parents think adolescence is a time of parental rejection and that they have little influence on teen-agers. It becomes very important for parents to open the communication channels because they can have an impact."

Abstinence Is a Realistic Goal

With the widespread failure of conventional sex ed and the growing success of abstinence education, advocates are poised to smash a paralyzing misconception about teenage sex: Although most parents would like their children to delay sex until marriage, they have been convinced that teenage sexual activity is inevitable and uncontrollable. This may come as a surprise to many, but raising teenagers to be sexually abstinent is a realistic goal. All the best research shows that parents are the single most important influence on whether their teens become sexually active. By some estimates, unfortunately, just 10 to 15 percent of today's youth have discussed sex with their parents, even though more than half of sexually active teens, according to a Roper Starch Survey, wish they could.

Kristine Napier, *Policy Review*, May/June 1997.

Research like this may not end the controversy over how we teach sex ed in schools (indeed, the study authors believe their findings aren't relevant to that debate). But at the very least they do suggest that parents with traditional values are not, as experts routinely portray them, an obstacle in the war against teen pregnancy, but one of our most powerful weapons.

One hopeful message to parents comes through loud and clear: Despite TV, despite peer pressure, despite hormones, the single biggest influence on whether or not your teen has sex is you.

And don't let any "expert" convince you otherwise.

> "*Abstinence is a highly risky philosophy in which to put our entire trust.*"

Teaching Abstinence Puts Teens at Risk of Pregnancy and Sexually Transmitted Diseases

M. Joycelyn Elders

In the following viewpoint, former U.S. surgeon general M. Joycelyn Elders maintains that sexual education programs promoting abstinence fail to recognize that most teenagers are having sex and therefore need protection against pregnancy and sexually transmitted diseases. The refusal to educate teens about condoms, she claims, places teenagers at a serious risk of contracting AIDS and other sexually transmitted diseases.

As you read, consider the following questions:

1. According to statistics cited by Elders, how many children and youths died of AIDS in 1996?
2. In Elders's opinion, why is abstinence a "highly risky philosophy"?
3. According to the author, why do European teenagers have lower rates of sexually transmitted diseases than teens in the United States?

Reprinted from Call to Arms, "Respect Your Elders!" by M. Joycelyn Elders, POZ, December 1997, by permission of POZ Publishing, New York, N.Y.

These days we confuse ignorance with innocence. Many adults believe (wrongly) that children are asexual, have no sexual thoughts, feelings or desires and shouldn't become aware of sex in any way before puberty. But in fact, sexual expression is coming earlier to teens, not because of loose morals or lack of values, but because children reach menses and puberty at an increasingly younger age. Yet by leaving them in the lurch rather than helping them understand the changes in their bodies, we punish our youth for what is literally beyond their control.

Few children today receive accurate, comprehensive health education at home; their mostly uninformed and anxious parents can't offer it. However, almost all children go to school, and it is there that they could most likely be prepared for a sexually healthy life. For we are losing our children and youth to disease, and it is time to act.

Teens Are Dying of AIDS

Consider these global statistics: In 1996, 1.5 million people, including 350,000 children and youths, died of AIDS. Of the 30 million people infected with HIV, 2.6 million—nearly one in 10—are adolescent or younger. Most new infections occur in people under 25, and about 80 percent of all adult infections occur through unprotected sexual intercourse—yet *condom* is still a naughty word in the United States.

Abstinence has been widely endorsed and heavily financed by the federal government. The Sexuality Information and Education Council of the United States (SIECUS) reported that all 50 states filed applications for their share of $50 million in federal funds for the welfare reform bill's abstinence-only education program. So while we refuse to support sexuality education, we try to legislate morals. But abstinence is a highly risky philosophy in which to put our entire trust. In his book *Solving America's Sexual Crisis*, sociologist Ira Reiss puts it best when he writes, "Vows of abstinence break more easily than do condoms."

Abstinence Programs Will Not Prevent New HIV Infections

Preventing new infections in the United States by promoting abstinence alone may never be accomplished, since three-quarters of all teen pregnancies are fathered by adult males. One study reveals a related—and very disturbing—trend: More adolescent girls than boys are diagnosed with HIV. According to the Centers for Disease Control and Prevention (CDC), 90 percent of the AIDS cases under age 20 are among girls. And these infections are acquired in childhood or early adolescence. These girls are generally not getting HIV from teen-age boys. In fact, many of the men responsible for infecting them are relatives.

Dan Wasserman ©1992 Boston Globe. Distributed by the Los Angeles Times Syndicate. Reprinted by permission.

It has been estimated that one in three girls is sexually abused by age 18, and one in four by age 14. These preteens—who cannot "just say no"—likely feel a special sense of shame and despair when their teachers emphasize that the only appropriate method for birth control and disease prevention is abstinence. Let's face it: Teen-agers are having sex, and they need condoms.

In 1997, Shari Lo, a California sophomore, won a trophy at her high school science fair for a project measuring condom reliability. She was on her way to the regional science-fair competition when the school superintendent disqualified her project, explaining that "because it is on condom reliability, it encourages safe sex. Our philosophy is abstinence, not safe sex."

THE NEED FOR COMPREHENSIVE SEX EDUCATION

It's true—albeit rarely stated so bluntly—that as a nation, we care more about philosophy than the lives of our youth. That's why U.S. teens have the highest rates of pregnancy, childbirth, abortion and HIV in the developed world—even though adolescent sexual activity and the age of initial sexual contact in other countries is similar to ours. Adolescents in countries such as Sweden, the Netherlands, Britain and France have much lower rates of Sexually Transmitted Diseases (STDs) and HIV than our own. Why? For one thing, all other developed nations have comprehensive health and sexuality education from kindergarten to grade 12. Discussion of contraception—including condoms—is widespread in the media, and universal health care makes birth control available and affordable. Finland's government sends out a brochure to every 16-year-old on his or her birthday that presents a positive depiction of adolescent sexuality, talks about responsibility and comes with a latex condom.

While our young are dying, we are quibbling over methods. Nationwide, one million teenage girls became pregnant in 1996, and half that number gave birth; three million youths got STDs. HIV infections and AIDS cases are both increasing fastest among adolescents.

Abstinence works for many of our youth. However, I'm not willing to just throw away all the rest for whom it does not work for one reason or another. We are at a low point in our nation's history in terms of caring for our children. We've tried legislating morals, and that didn't work. We've tried just saying no, and that didn't work. We've tried ignorance, and that didn't work. Why don't we try education? Let's end this shameful era by standing up and stepping out to save our precious children.

"If ... young girls were reliably
protected against pregnancy ...
young women would reach legal
adulthood prepared to make their
own reproductive choices in a more
mature way."

LONG-TERM CONTRACEPTIVE DEVICES CAN HELP PREVENT TEEN PREGNANCY

Margaret P. Battin

In the following viewpoint, Margaret P. Battin argues that placing adolescent girls on long-term contraceptive devices would avert all unintentional teenage pregnancies. One such device is Norplant, a contraceptive that is surgically placed in the arm and protects against pregnancy for up to five years. The use of Norplant or other long-term contraceptive devices, Battin contends, would effectively immunize girls against pregnancy until they made the choice to have children. Battin is a professor of medical ethics at the University of Utah School of Medicine.

As you read, consider the following questions:

1. In Battin's opinion, what is the present approach to the problem of teenage pregnancy?
2. How is the use of long-term contraception similar to an immunization against disease, in the author's opinion?
3. According to the author, what are the current means available for long-term contraception?

Reprinted from Margaret P. Battin, "A Better Approach to Adolescent Pregnancy," *Social Science and Medicine*, vol. 41, no. 9, 1995, by permission of Elsevier Science.

For all young women, pregnancy and childbearing is physiologically riskier in the earliest postpubescent years than later. Very early pregnancy is associated with higher rates of both maternal and infant morbidity and mortality. In many cultures, pregnancy in early adolescence is regarded as socially disruptive, especially when no father is known or present and the young mother is the child's sole means of support; it is seen as perpetuating a cycle of poverty. Early pregnancy is often associated with higher rates of malnourishment and inadequate schooling for the child, less education and less economic independence for the mother and higher rates of disturbance in the home.

. . . The individual, social and global risks of very early childbearing are substantial. Given the very large number of adolescent pregnancies that occur annually and the multiple grounds on which postponement of them may seem desirable, we must ask whether there may not be a better strategy for prevention or reduction of unplanned adolescent pregnancy. I would like to propose a thought-experiment—a conjecture—about a better way of approaching the matter of adolescent pregnancy. This may seem outrageous; but because it reveals so much about our current attitudes, I think it is important to have it carefully considered.

USING EDUCATION TO PREVENT TEENAGE PREGNANCY

Clearly, what is done now does not work, at least not everywhere. The prevention of teenage pregnancy, at least in those countries which attempt it, is currently approached mainly by education: adolescent girls are informed of the benefits of avoiding pregnancy and warned of its risks, and are provided with information about the behavioural and contraceptive means of doing so. . . . If education about pregnancy prevention is adequate, it is assumed, teenagers will remain abstinent, or provide themselves with contraceptives or insist that their partners do so.

In some countries, this works well: in the Netherlands and Sweden for example, the rate of teenage pregnancy is very low. In other countries, such as the United States, it is less successful: the rate of teenage pregnancy is high, the highest in the developed world. This is often attributed to differences in sex education: in the United States, unlike the northern European countries, formal sex education is often grossly inadequate . . . and cultural pressures . . . often favour rather than discourage teenage pregnancy.

In some countries, adolescent pregnancy is effectively prevented not by education but by rigid sex-segregation and severe sanctions if it occurs. In other countries, especially in the developing world, pregnancy during adolescence is common.

In many cultures in sub-Saharan Africa, for instance, traditional cultural patterns encourage very early marriage and immediate childbearing. . . . Pregnancy during adolescence varies widely among cultures but it is nevertheless frequent on a global scale. . . .

Is there a better way to approach adolescent pregnancy, given its consequences, its risks and its ubiquitousness—a better way than ineffectual reliance on education or rigid sex segregation? . . . What if it were arranged that adolescent girls, from puberty through 17 (or, in most places, legal adulthood), could not become pregnant unless they made a deliberate, conscious choice to do so? How would this change their prospects, their offspring's prospects and the prospects of their families, societies and the world?

THE BENEFITS OF LONG-TERM CONTRACEPTION

This is conjecture only in one sense: we are probably politically incapable of making it happen. But it is not merely a thought-experiment in another sense: after all, we already have the technology available now that would make this possible. This technology, not usually distinguished from its predecessors, involves long-term contraception which is 'automatic' in its function: it works all the time regardless of what the user does. Unlike short-term modalities such as the condom, the diaphragm, the sponge, and various herbal potions and powders, true 'automatic' long-term contraception provides continuous pregnancy prevention without any further action on the part of the user: without having to obtain it, store it, apply it or activate it, ingest it or insert it, either beforehand or at the time of sex—indeed, without having to do anything at all. (It is this feature of user-independence that makes true long-term contraception ideal for young or inexperienced users.)

Such a strategy would be like immunising youngsters against other health risks: tetanus, diphtheria, pertussis, polio—except that long-term contraception is not permanent and can be immediately reversed when the user wishes. Nor does such contraception in any way interfere with adult reproductive capacity; it is just that adolescents do not become pregnant unless they actively choose to do so. . . .

CURRENT TECHNOLOGIES IN LONG-TERM CONTRACEPTION

At the moment, there are just two contraceptives for women which are sufficiently long-term to remain effective throughout adolescence but nevertheless permit a complete and immediate return to fertility if the user wishes—the subdermal, lev-onorgestrel implant (Norplant) and the intra-uterine device (IUD). . . . Norplant is effective for years; the contemporary IUD is effective for eight to ten years. Both have excellent reliability and safety records, though both involve some disadvantages, in-cluding side effects and culturally unacceptable consequences like altered bleeding patterns or invasion of modesty. There are no reliable, safe, long-term contraceptive technologies yet avail-able for males. . . . Other long-acting female contraceptives now on the market, such as Depo-Provera and, when taken continu-ously, the Pill, still require user co-operation: this means re-membering and obtaining repeat applications, not a foolproof expectation for teenagers.

THE USE OF NORPLANT WOULD REDUCE TEEN PREGNANCIES

Abstinence is the best goal of social policy. But the harsh fact is that we have neither the social will nor the practical tools to achieve it. Meanwhile, each year teenagers have another 400,000 abortions, and 300,000 babies out of wedlock. . . .

Norplant's very effectiveness would lead to a marginal increase in sexual activity among teens, and thus to a concomitant in-crease in sexually transmitted diseases (which Norplant does not prevent). But on the other side of the social ledger, widespread use of Norplant would sharply reduce the number of abortions and babies born out of wedlock.

Douglas J. Besharov, *National Review*, August 9, 1993.

But this conjecture . . . is not limited to the currently available technologies. Improvements in the two current truly 'automatic' technologies, Norplant and the IUD, and other newly developing modalities allow us to imagine a world in which reliance on ed-ucational strategies of variable (but generally low) effectiveness for preventing teen pregnancy is no longer necessary. . . . Every adolescent has [protection], just as every adolescent is immu-nised against polio whether they expect to be exposed or not. In-deed, the use of such contraception would be entirely indepen-dent of sex: initiated at puberty, it would simply be a basic protective feature of their lives. Of course, sexually active adoles-cents would still need to concern themselves about sexually transmitted diseases, and use condoms if appropriate in addition, but they would not need to worry about unwanted pregnancy.

Of course, adolescents could still have children if they wished to do so. Pregnancy would simply require a positive choice to have the contraceptive device neutralised or removed. Nevertheless, up to the time of legal adulthood, adolescents would be protected from incurring pregnancy in involuntary, inadequately informed, impulsive or unthinking ways—just the ways in which many, perhaps most, adolescent pregnancies occur.

Think about this conjecture carefully. Consider the physical and psychological costs of unwanted, unplanned adolescent pregnancy to the young girls themselves, to their partners, families and social groupings; then consider the larger social costs to their societies, and finally consider the strains in terms of global population and resource pressures. Of course there are often benefits to early pregnancy. But if it were routine that young girls were reliably protected against pregnancy they did not intend, many of the costs would disappear, the benefits could be maintained for those who chose them, and in general, young women would reach legal adulthood prepared to make their own reproductive choices in a more mature way. This would have incalculable repercussions for gender equality; it could alleviate social friction over the issue of abortion, since pregnancy would all be by choice; and it would have a very favourable impact on poverty-perpetuating and population pressures—all without violating any woman's right to have the number of children she wished.

Too bad we aren't developing fully reliable, perfectly safe, side-effect-free long-term contraceptive technologies for both women and men at a faster rate. This would permit a change in human reproduction control from reliance on short-term methods to the routine use of long-term 'automatic' contraception: it would, so to speak, change the default mode in human reproduction—choices about reproduction would no longer be negative choices to avoid children, but positive choices to have them. This simple change—from a negative choice to prevent pregnancy (which is what our sex-education programmes ask of teenagers now) to a positive choice to seek pregnancy—may seem a very minor change in decisional structure, based on a small difference in contraceptive technology, but it is one with incalculable consequences for women, men and the world.

"To [implant Norplant in teenage girls] would be to . . . state publicly that there are no social standards or sanctions with respect to the sexual activity of young people."

LONG-TERM CONTRACEPTIVE DEVICES PROMOTE TEEN PROMISCUITY

Richard John Neuhaus

In the following viewpoint, Richard John Neuhaus responds to a proposal by Douglas J. Besharov to grant teenagers easy access to the contraceptive Norplant, a long-term contraceptive device that is surgically implanted in the arm and retains its effectiveness for up to five years. Neuhaus maintains that granting access to Norplant would send a message to teenagers that sex is expected of them, thereby vastly increasing teen promiscuity. Neuhaus is the religion editor for *National Review*, a conservative monthly magazine.

As you read, consider the following questions:

1. How does Norplant reduce teenagers' incentives to remain virgins, according to Neuhaus?
2. In Neuhaus's words, what message does the use of Norplant send to teenagers in the inner cities?
3. According to the author, what are the dangerous effects of teenage promiscuity?

Reprinted, by permission, from Richard John Neuhaus, "A Better Choice," *National Review*, August 9, 1993; ©1993 by National Review, Inc., 215 Lexington Ave., New York, NY 10016.

M r. Douglas J. Besharov [in his proposal to grant teenagers easy access to Norplant] asks us, "Which is worse: the possibility of a marginal increase in sexual activity? Or losing the opportunity to reduce abortions and out-of-wedlock births by 10, 20, or even 30 per cent? To ask the question is to answer it." I have asked the question, and it is by no means answered. The alternatives he poses are misleading.

Given the figure of a million teenage pregnancies, a 10 per cent reduction by the use of Norplant would require 100,000 implantations. In either case, it's an ambitious program. Presumably the program is voluntary and hundreds of thousands of teenage girls (the proposal does put all the responsibility on the girls) would want to have a minor surgical procedure that would contraceptively equip them for sexual intercourse. Presumably also, the parents would have some say in this and would agree to having their daughters thus equipped. Presumably yet further, one result would be "the possibility of a marginal increase in sexual activity."

A Substantial Increase in Teenage Sex

I suggest that the result would be the near certainty of a *substantial* increase in sexual intercourse among teenagers. If so, that would mean also an increase in abortions and single-parent children. The problems that the proposal intends to resolve would be greatly exacerbated.

Of course we do not know for sure until it is tried. There are many perilous things that should not be tried. We should not under public auspices try implanting Norplant in teenage girls. To do so would be to try something that possibly no society has tried before: to state publicly that there are no social standards or sanctions with respect to the sexual activity of young people. It might be objected that we are already making that statement by distributing condoms in public schools. Just so. Which is why condom distribution is a dumb idea, and far from settled policy in most schools.

Giving Up on Discouraging Teen Promiscuity

Mr. Besharov says that abstinence is the best goal "for younger teens especially." (At 15 you can't do it but at 16 you can?) He adds, "But the harsh fact is that we have neither the social will nor the practical tools to achieve [the goal of abstinence]." I do not know what he means by "practical tools," but presumably we do not have means of discouraging and encouraging certain behaviors among young people. Parents have never succeeded in controlling totally the behavior of their children, which is just as well. But if Mr. Besharov is suggesting that parents—and churches and schools—should give up on discouraging sexual promiscuity and encouraging abstinence, his is even more of a counsel of despair than I had at first thought.

The critical reference is to "social will." To whom, one may ask, belong the wills that make up this social will? Teenagers, parents, brothers, sisters, pastors, teachers, school boards, aunts, and uncles—each, one by one, can have a will with respect to teenage sexuality. Or perhaps the suggestion is that most people who are in a position to influence teenagers really do not care about what they do sexually. The survey research data do not support that suggestion. But even if most people did not care, that does not mean that we should adopt public policies premised upon not caring. Mr. Besharov cares. He obviously cares about abortion and out-of-wedlock children, and by implication he cares about teenage fornication (he calls it an evil). I have never met the "social will," but I have met many people who care very much about their children's sexual behavior.

But Mr. Besharov, along with many others, is discouraged about the possibility of encouraging abstinence from sexual intercourse. The discouragement is understandable. Many in the media, entertainment, and educational establishments proclaim that abstinence is unnatural, chastity is unattainable, and virginity is a form of sexual deviance. And yet, in such a social climate, at least one half of teenage girls are virgins. It seems quite remarkable. Many in the other half have had sex only once or twice, while many more, those who have been very "sexually active," know that what they have done is not right.

Encouraging Teens Who Want to Abstain

Let us stipulate for argument's sake that 25 per cent of teenage girls are sexually promiscuous and think there is nothing wrong with that. Why should we agree with them by adopting policies that declare that the sexual behavior of young people is a matter of public indifference? Why should we not, rather, encourage the 75 per cent who want to do the right thing, even if they do not always behave as they know they ought? When it comes to doing the right thing, incentives and disincentives are always in fragile balance. Those who want to do the right thing need all the support that they can get. Girls in particular need support in resisting predatory males.

Consider 16-year-old Thelma who has her Norplant in place. Her reasons for saying no are sharply reduced. She is equipped for sex. Her school and, presumably, her parents have said that they *expect* her to have sexual intercourse. Saying no seems arbitrary, irrational, and downright unfriendly. If through public policy we declare that we expect teenagers to be sexually promiscuous, that it is the normal thing, it is reasonable to suppose that more teenagers will be sexually promiscuous. If, on the other hand, we make it clear that we expect abstinence, chastity, and self-command, virtue might be given a helping hand.

CONTRACEPTION SHOULD NOT REPLACE EDUCATION

[Norplant's] magic technology replaces individual decision-making and discourages responsible attitudes regarding sexual behaviour, not least on the part of men.

This is undesirable both from an ethical and practical point of view. In the absence of [sexual] education, for example, why suppose that behavioural patterns formed when it was not necessary to assume responsibility for reproductive choices will automatically be replaced by mature behaviour when the long-term contraceptive is withdrawn? How would women have been prepared to make mature choices in the absence of education?

Rosa N. Geldstein and Edith A. Pantelides, *Reproductive Health Matters*, November 1, 1996.

Or we can give up. We can, perhaps implicitly but with a powerful social effect, agree with the minority (maybe the small minority) of teenagers who are sexually promiscuous and think there is nothing wrong with that. But, it might be objected, Norplant would be used selectively. It would not be a general statement of approval with respect to teenage promiscuity since it would be given only to those girls who already are "sexually active."

Anyone who takes that objection seriously has been on a long vacation from American reality. Norplant would be administered, as it is said, on a non-discriminatory basis, meaning there is no room for discriminations between good and bad, right and wrong. There must be, as policy guidelines would make clear, no "judgmental" connotation attached to getting a Norplant—the rules of self-esteem require that. In sum, great effort would be expended in making sure it is understood that Norplant and the sexual promiscuity it is intended to facilitate are perfectly acceptable.

RACIST CONNOTATIONS OF NORPLANT POLICIES

To be sure, many Americans think it is more acceptable for "their" teenagers than for ours. The racist caricature of inner-city black teenagers as incorrigibly rutting animals is no part of Mr. Besharov's argument, but it is an undeniable part of the public discussion of Norplant, condom distribution, and related policies. Those who live at the bottom margin of society, where the fragility of behavioral norms is most pronounced, are most in need of encouragement. What they do not need is a message from the larger society, conveyed through public policies such as the use of Norplant, that nothing better is expected of them.

There are other considerations that Mr. Besharov does not address adequately. He touches all too lightly, for example, on the epidemic of venereal diseases (now called sexually transmitted diseases or STDs). Some 65 per cent of STDs are found among teenagers, some of them resulting in sterility or even in death. Norplant is of no help in resisting STDs, and the sexual behavior that it facilitates is the very means of infection. Mr. Besharov also neglects the documented relationship between sexual promiscuity among teenagers and failing grades, drug and alcohol abuse, increased suicide rates, and other "at risk" behavior. The entire society has a large stake in teenagers growing up to form stable and healthy marriages. Policies that have the effect of "normalizing" promiscuity make that goal much less likely.

Mr. Besharov notes the explosion of abortion rates after the 1973 *Roe vs. Wade* decision. Abortion is legal, many thought, therefore abortion is all right and therefore abortion rates soared. But policies and their consequences can move in other directions. For instance, we know that, in states that require parental consent for abortion, both teenage abortion rates and teenage pregnancy rates fall dramatically. What changes once can be changed again. "Each year," Mr. Besharov writes, "teenagers have another 400,000 abortions and 300,000 babies out of wedlock." There is nothing inevitable about that. It was not the case 25 years ago and it need not be the case ten years from now.

The Norplant proposal leans in one direction, aiming to contain the damage of the allegedly inevitable, and I suggest we should lean in the other, determined to reduce both abortions and out-of-wedlock births by challenging the sexual license that is the source of both.

> "In the case of teen-age pregnancies, all that is needed is thorough and systematic enforcement of laws pertaining to statutory rape."

ENFORCING STATUTORY RAPE LAWS CAN HELP REDUCE TEEN PREGNANCY

Ralph deToledano

Statutory rape laws prohibit adults from engaging in sex with minors and, in some cases, forbid teenagers from having sex with each other. In the following viewpoint, Ralph deToledano promotes the vigorous enforcement of these laws as an effective way to reduce the incidence of teenage pregnancy. If males knew they faced fines or imprisonment for having sex with teenage girls, he contends, a significant number of teenage pregnancies would be averted. DeToledano is a syndicated columnist.

As you read, consider the following questions:

1. In the author's opinion, if a teenage girl becomes pregnant, what should she be required to do?
2. According to deToledano, what should the government require of males who father illegitimate children?
3. How does deToledano characterize the "New Morality"?

Reprinted from Ralph deToledano, "Teen-Age Mothers: Lots of Talk, Little Action," *Conservative Chronicle*, August 28, 1996, by permission of Ralph deToledano and Creators Syndicate.

Teen-age pregnancies, as well as those of women 19–23, continue to be both a social problem and a drain on federal, state and municipal budgets. The annual rate of these pregnancies continues to zoom—some 5 percent a year—but all that Congress and state legislatures have done about it is to wring their collective hands. Now there will be more viewing with alarm as a 24-member bipartisan congressional [committee] ponders the situation, seeking to throw more laws and more money at the problem.

"The explosion of out-of-wedlock teen births is a moral crisis that threatens to undermine our nation," says Rep. Nita Lowry, a leader of the Congressional Advisory Panel to the National Campaign to Reduce Teen-Age Pregnancy. But Robert Rector, an analyst at the Heritage Foundation, adds: "The reality is, most of out-of-wedlock births occur to women age 19 to 23—and this is what cuts into the taxpayer's pocket the most."

So we will get more talk, but little action. And the fact is that out-of-wedlock pregnancies could be cut down dramatically without passage of a single new law.

ENFORCING STATUTORY RAPE LAWS

In the case of teen-age pregnancies, all that is needed is thorough and systematic enforcement of laws pertaining to statutory rape. A girl of 16 and under has, by law, been raped, whether she consented to or even initiated the sex act. She should be required to name and testify against the male, of any age, who should be prosecuted for rape and given the maximum penalty. Once upon a time, this was done routinely, but the liberal bleeding hearts have tied the hands of police, prosecutors and the government agencies that handle and subsidize these pregnancies.

If these predatory males knew for certain that they would face prison and fines for every casual roll in the hay, you would see a tremendous decline in the teen-age pregnancies that result. In addition to fines and imprisonment, these men can be compelled to support their illegitimate offspring, which would free government from becoming surrogate parents.

As for the women in the 19 to 23 age range, they too can be required to name the father of their child, to the attending physician. An unwed mother who goes on welfare should be required to name the father of her child, and he could be traced through his Social Security number if he became a fugitive from his parental responsibility. He cannot be made to marry the woman he has made pregnant, but he can be compelled to support his child. With this over their heads, men would be less prone to indulge in casual and irresponsible liaisons. The financial burdens of out-of-wedlock sex would pass from the welfare system to the individual involved.

A RETURN TO RESPONSIBILITY

One would think that the women's-fibbers and the organized feminists would be gung-ho for the enforcement of now-existent laws to protect girls and young women from what is largely their victimization. It would do far more for the status of women than the campaign against domestic violence.

ADULT MEN ARE CAUSING TEEN PREGNANCIES

The problem with teen sex is not simply that teens are having sex. Adults, in disturbing numbers, are having sex with teens. . . . Federal and state surveys suggest that adult males are the fathers of some two-thirds of the babies born to teenage girls. According to the Alan Guttmacher Institute, 39 percent of 15-year-old mothers say the fathers of their babies are 20 years old or older. For 17-year-old teenage moms, 55 percent of the fathers are adults; for 19-year-olds, it is 78 percent.

Joseph P. Shapiro, U.S. News & World Report, August 14, 1995.

But we live in a time, brought on by liberal ideology, in which all the talk is of rights and none of responsibilities. In the past, men and women flouted the moral and social standards of the community. But if it ended in trouble, they did not go running to a governmental Daddy to bail them out. If a man got a woman pregnant, there were social pressures to make him marry her or to provide for the child. That is, if the man could not push the woman into having an abortion.

THE "NEW MORALITY"

But the New Morality, stemming from Havelock Ellis, Freud and feminist "liberationism," has cheapened human relations and made sex about as significant as chewing gum. People have a "right" to act as irresponsibly as they wish—and then to send the bill to the government. Men and women are "entitled" to having society pay for their carelessness—and the cost be damned.

To do otherwise is to destroy the individual's "self-esteem." To listen to the New Moralists, social restraints are a form of fascism—and to be concerned over what people do in the privacy of the bedroom or the parked car, no matter what the cost to society or to the individuals involved, is unconstitutional and a violation of the Rights of Man.

So we will have congressional commissions and perhaps hearings by Senate and House Committees. There will be much alarmist talk. But nothing will be done to enforce the laws now on the books for fear that it will upset the American Civil Liberties Union, Hillary Clinton and the liberal media. And the incidence of out-of-wedlock pregnancies, paid for by your taxes and mine, will increase.

And the wringing of hands, the viewing with alarm, will go on, ad infinitum and ad nauseam, until people begin really to care.

> "As a remedy for teen pregnancy, . . .
> the crusade against statutory rape is
> . . . impractical."

ENFORCING STATUTORY RAPE LAWS WILL NOT REDUCE TEEN PREGNANCY

Catherine Elton

Enforcing statutory rape laws, which prohibit adults from having sex with minors, has been promoted by some as an effective method for deterring teenage pregnancy. In the following viewpoint, Catherine Elton asserts that the enforcement of statutory rape laws would only avert a small percentage of teenage pregnancies. Furthermore, she contends, cases of statutory rape are nearly impossible to prosecute because teenage girls are often reluctant to testify against their older boyfriends. Elton is a writer for the *New Republic*, a weekly magazine that offers opinions on political and social issues.

As you read, consider the following questions:

1. According to statistics cited by Elton, how many fifteen- to seventeen-year-old unmarried teenage girls have babies fathered by men at least four years older?
2. What does Elton propose as an appropriate alternative in some cases to enforcing statutory rape laws?
3. Why do advocates for teen mothers worry about the enforcement of statutory rape laws, in the author's opinion?

When a Wisconsin prosecutor charged 19-year-old Kevin Gillson with sexual assault for impregnating his 15-year-old girlfriend, it was widely seen as a case of prosecutorial discretion gone awry. "The insanity of this so-called abuse prosecution speaks for itself," the *St. Petersburg Times* editorialized. Noting that Gillson's name would be entered into a national registry for sex offenders even though he planned to marry his girlfriend and help raise the child, *The Milwaukee Journal Sentinel*, like many observers, pleaded "for judicial mercy."

But while the Gillson case was extreme, it was nonetheless emblematic of a new trend: fighting teen pregnancy through tougher statutory rape laws. California, Delaware, Florida, and Georgia have all passed legislation beefing up existing laws prohibiting sex with girls under the age of consent. In his State of the State address, Republican California Governor Pete Wilson declared, "It's not macho to get a teenager pregnant, but if you lack the decency to understand this yourself we'll give you a year to think about it in county jail." Wilson has dedicated $8.4 million to the Statutory Rape Vertical Prosecution program, which now boasts 827 convictions. (Prior to this, one California official told me, prosecuting statutory rape "just wasn't happening.") The federal government has jumped on the bandwagon, too: the 1996 Welfare Reform Act contained a provision calling for states to "aggressively enforce statutory rape laws," while the attorney general has called the issue a "high priority."

An "Epidemic" of Adult Men Preying on Teenage Girls

The trend's genesis lies in a handful of studies, published in 1995 while the nation was knee-deep in the welfare reform debate, which revealed that as many as two-thirds of teenage girls who became pregnant did so by adult men. As the two-thirds number became famous, politicians suggested what they thought was an obvious remedy: prosecute the "predatory males," not merely to set an example but also to keep them from striking again. But applying this theory has proven far more difficult than the politicians ever imagined. There are clearly cases in which relationships between older men and younger women are inappropriate, but determining which relationships fall into that category requires moral judgments about which Americans are sincerely, and deeply, divided. Even in the most egregious cases, criminalizing the behavior may be too extreme a response.

To understand why, go back to the studies for a moment. They did not really show—as many politicians seemed to think—that there was an epidemic of older men preying upon school-aged girls. According to a study by the Urban Institute, a well-respected authority on these matters, 62 percent of teen pregnancies (births to 15- to 19-year-olds) involve 18- or 19-year-old mothers. What's more, only 27 percent of babies born to girls who are 15, 16, or 17 are fathered by men at least five years older; 23 percent of the pregnant 15- to 17-year-olds with partners five or more years older are married when they give birth. The Urban Institute concluded that "only 8 percent [of teen pregnancies] involved unmarried women aged 15 to 17 and men who were at least five years older," and that only 13 percent of all pregnancies to unmarried 15- to 17-year-olds are fathered by men at least four years older.

STATUTORY RAPE LAWS ARE APPLIED UNEQUALLY

Law enforcement officials apply the [statutory rape] law principally against two groups: men, frequently older, who have sex with girls from "good homes"; and minority men, who are punished if they commit the crime of having sex with white women or impregnate a woman of color under circumstances that add to the welfare rolls.

Richard Delgato, *ABA Journal*, August 1996.

Even within this small group, prosecutors are finding it hard to get convictions, for it's often not clear whether the girls are really "victims." "Juries have trouble with these cases because they think teenagers lie, they think she manipulated him, and jurors think she looks older," says Sharon Elstein, coordinator of a forthcoming American Bar Association (ABA) study on the issue. "They wonder why the court is wasting its time."

While the relationship between, say, a 15-year-old girl and a 21-year-old man may strike a prosecutor as inherently coercive, it doesn't instantly resonate as criminal among a jury of peers. "When you meet the 20-year-old and the 13-year-old you are surprised," says Mike Males, an author of one of the first studies to pinpoint the two-thirds figure. "Thirteen-year-olds are portrayed as gum-chewing, braces-wearing twits and the 20-year-olds are supposed to be more mature. Very often this is not the case."

Of course, many times the girls don't see themselves as victims, and this is enough to scare off many prosecutors: it's hard to convict when the victim blows kisses to the defendant or leaves the courtroom holding his hand. But the ABA found that one-quarter of prosecutors it surveyed would pursue action regardless. Rick Trunfio, an assistant district attorney in Syracuse,

New York, is one such prosecutor: he had been aggressively taking on these cases even before it became fashionable in the media. In a community of 500,000, his office prosecutes 100 to 150 cases per year; 80 percent of the time, he wins some kind of a conviction (sometimes to a lesser crime). Not prosecuting because of uncooperative victims is, in Trunfio's eyes, a "cop-out." "That's what subpoenas are for," he says without hesitation, noting that he's willing to subpoena not just a victim but her diaries and her love letters, too.

ENFORCING STATUTORY RAPE LAWS IS IMPRACTICAL

Trunfio and other zealous prosecutors liken their cause to the fight against domestic violence. There was, after all, a time when society would refuse to prosecute a man who beat his wife because the victim did not want to cooperate. But in some teen sex cases, it's probably more appropriate to encourage the "victim" to marry the older male—and get out of her parents' unstable home—than to prosecute the father. During the summer of 1996, for example, in Orange County, California, social service workers and a juvenile court even recommended a pregnant 13-year-old marry her 20-year-old boyfriend because it provided more stability than her current lifestyle of skipping school and abusing drugs. "We are hearing these guys are exploitative, opportunistic predators," says Elstein, "but it's not all like that. Sometimes this is the best thing that's ever happened to her."

Perhaps, as Trunfio argues, there is something inherently exploitative about a relationship between an older man or boy and a young teenage girl. But advocates for teen mothers also worry that, if the state really begins to crack down on statutory rape, girls will stop coming in for prenatal care because they fear somebody might report their boyfriends.

And then, of course, there is the concern about disproportionate punishment for men. Since statutory rape is a sex crime, many of those convicted must register as sexual offenders. But is it really fair to lump a 20-year-old who got a 15-year-old pregnant together with child molesters? As a political rallying cry, prosecuting statutory rape offered politicians a chance to attack a modern-day problem with a traditional sounding solution. As a remedy for teen pregnancy, however, the crusade against statutory rape is not only impractical, but it often has a far different impact than intended. "[T]hanks to the court system," Gillson's young fiancée said in a statement read into the court record, "I have lost the love of my life and the father of my unborn baby."

| *"Welfare is illegitimacy's economic life support system."*

ENDING WELFARE WILL HELP REDUCE TEEN PREGNANCY

William J. Bennett and Peter Wehner

William J. Bennett and Peter Wehner argue in the following viewpoint that the welfare system encourages out-of-wedlock births, many of which are to teenage mothers. If welfare benefits were eliminated, the authors maintain, the number of young single women having babies would fall dramatically. Bennett is a codirector of Empower America, a free market political advocacy organization, and the author of *The Book of Virtues*. Wehner is the director of policy at Empower America.

As you read, consider the following questions:

1. According to the authors, what important moral principle is behind the proposed policy to end welfare?
2. What evidence do Bennett and Wehner offer for the failure of the welfare system?
3. In the authors' opinion, what should be the point of welfare reform?

Reprinted from William J. Bennett and Peter Wehner, "Let's Outlaw Welfare for Unmarried Mothers," *Newsday*, February 3, 1994, by permission of the authors.

Republicans should propose legislation that ends welfare for anyone having a child out of wedlock. Our preference is to end, one year after the legislation is passed, all forms of economic support for single mothers who have new children. [The Welfare Reform bill of 1996 required that teenage mothers live at home or attend school in order to collect welfare benefits, but did not abolish temporary aid to single mothers.]

These would include Aid to Families with Dependent Children, subsidized housing and food stamps, an end to all forms of assistance for those single mothers currently on welfare, an end to visitation rights for illegitimate fathers and a change in tax codes to make them more favorable to marriage and children. The specifics are less important than the end game; somewhere soon we want welfare to end, and when it does we can judge these policies, and their broad social consequences, against reality.

HAVING CHILDREN OUT OF WEDLOCK IS WRONG

These proposed policy changes are based on an important moral principle: Having children out of wedlock is wrong—not simply economically unwise for the individuals involved or a financial burden on society, but morally wrong.

Even Secretary of Health and Human Services Donna Shalala, she of impeccable liberal credentials, said in an interview: "I don't like to put this in moral terms, but I do believe that having children out of wedlock is just wrong."

By the year 2000, according to the most reliable projections, 40 percent of all American births and 80 percent of minority births will be illegitimate. These numbers have frightening social implications. Welfare may not cause illegitimacy, but it does make it economically practical. There is hardly any question illegitimacy rates would fall—probably dramatically—if aid-to-dependent-children payments were stopped. Welfare is illegitimacy's economic life support system.

THE WELFARE SYSTEM SHOULD BE ENDED

Social scientist Charles Murray, in a 1993 *Wall Street Journal* article, went beyond the unwed-mother issue. He called for ending the current welfare system outright. His views had an explosive effect, and set off a chain reaction that transformed the welfare debate. We are now at one of those rare political moments when a fundamental, even radical, and positive change in public policy is possible.

That reform of this magnitude is possible can be explained

largely by widespread acceptance of overwhelming empirical evidence: The current welfare system is a complete failure. Over the last three decades, we have spent enormous sums of money on welfare programs, and what do we have to show for it? An underclass that is much larger, more violent and more poorly educated and consisting of many more single-parent families.

Reprinted by permission of Chuck Asay and Creators Syndicate.

Reaction to Murray's article was overwhelmingly favorable, including positive reaction from some unlikely places. Here is what President Bill Clinton said in an interview about welfare's fiercest and most prominent critic:

"[Murray] did the country a great service. He and I have often disagreed, but I think his analysis is essentially right. . . . There's no question that [ending welfare payments to single mothers] would work. The question is . . . is it morally right?"

Clinton's embrace of the Murray analysis means the intellectual debate over welfare policy is essentially over; we are now debating the relative merits of changing the current system vs. dismantling it. . . .

WELFARE ENCOURAGES ILLEGITIMACY

The point [of welfare reform] is not to ensure tougher work provisions and job training; rather, it is to go after a system that fosters illegitimacy and its attendant social pathologies. Making adoption easier is an essential and compassionate part of this effort. Adoption is the best alternative we have to protecting a child's interest in a post-welfare world. The demand for adoption is virtually unlimited, but society has made adoption exceedingly difficult. Lifting restrictions on interracial adoption and easing age limitations for adoptive parents will help ensure that large numbers of children will be adopted into good, stable, loving homes. And for older children, we must invest generously in the kind of orphanages and group homes that provide order and care.

Ending welfare in this way is prudent, humane and politically smart. It would be prudent because the social science evidence is in: Illegitimacy is the surest road to economic poverty and social decay. And welfare subsidizes and sustains illegitimacy. . . .

The current welfare system is the most pernicious government program of the last quarter-century. We have lost large parts of an entire generation because of the human wreckage left in its wake. Enough is enough. It's time to pull the plug.

VIEWPOINT

> "[Eliminating welfare] may have the perverse and unintended consequence of encouraging some of the conditions . . . associated with teen pregnancy—principally poverty and and family dysfunction."

ENDING WELFARE WILL NOT REDUCE TEEN PREGNANCY

Kristin A. Moore

In the following viewpoint, Kristin A. Moore contends that abolishing the welfare system will do nothing to prevent teenage pregnancy. In fact, the author claims, as welfare benefits have been scaled back, teenage pregnancy has increased—a statistic that defies the notion that welfare encourages teen pregnancies. Moore is executive director of Child Trends, Inc., a research organization dedicated to studying children, youth, and families.

As you read, consider the following questions:

1. According to Moore, what four factors promote teenage pregnancy?
2. What does the author cite as two consequences of cutting welfare to teenage mothers?
3. In the author's opinion, how should long-term welfare dependency of teenage mothers be discouraged?

Reprinted from Kristin A. Moore, "Welfare Bill Won't Stop Teenage Pregnancy," *The Christian Science Monitor*, Opinion/Essays, December 18, 1995, by permission of the author.

Among the most controversial [issues in the United States] is the question of what role welfare plays in encouraging teenage pregnancy and childbearing. About one-half of women on welfare were teens when they had their first child. In general, teenage mothers are much less likely than their childless peers to complete high school and much more likely to need long-term support.

Does this mean welfare promotes teen pregnancy? Those who say yes argue you get more of what you subsidize. But if this were the case, one would expect teen birth rates to have declined in recent years, as welfare benefits have shrunk. Instead, births to teenagers have increased. The argument that welfare encourages teen births also suggests that European countries, which offer more generous benefits than the US, should have higher rates of teenage childbirths. Yet they don't.

What Promotes Teen Pregnancy?

So if welfare doesn't promote teen pregnancy, what does? Overwhelmingly, evidence points to four underlying factors, none of which are addressed by cutting welfare to teenage parents. These factors are: 1) early school failure, 2) early behavior problems, 3) poverty, and 4) family dysfunction. Study after study finds a strong link between these four conditions and early sexual activity, teenage pregnancy, and adolescent parenthood.

As early as elementary school, children who have trouble in school often become frustrated and exhibit behavior problems. As school success becomes less attainable, they may see little value in playing by the rules that help other students get ahead. Over time, some grow susceptible to dangerous influences in their neighborhoods and schools and to negative messages in the news media and popular culture. Too often, the results are drug and alcohol use, violence, and early and unprotected sex, which can lead to teen pregnancy.

Poor children, in particular, may feel less hopeful about the future and may therefore see less reason than more-affluent children to delay childbearing until after marriage—or at least until they are financially able to support a child. Data on teen pregnancy and childbearing consistently show that adolescents in poor families and communities tend to initiate sexual intercourse at a younger age, to use contraceptives less effectively, and to have more unintended pregnancies.

Finally, children in dysfunctional families are at higher risk of early pregnancy. Their parents often fail to provide adequate supervision, to communicate effectively with their children, to teach strong values, and to educate them about how and why to delay sex and parenthood. Most dramatically, severely dysfunctional families may fail to protect their daughters from unwanted sexual advances. Increasingly, studies indicate many girls' initial sexual experiences are coercive. A majority of girls whose first sexual experiences occurred before age 15 report that these incidents were not voluntary.

CUTTING WELFARE WILL NOT INFLUENCE TEEN BEHAVIOR

If you have ever spent time around adolescents, you know that long-range planning is not one of their strong points. It is ridiculous to believe that denying welfare benefits to [teenage] mothers . . . will cut the rate of illegitimate births.

Cynthia Tucker, *Liberal Opinion*, January 30, 1995.

As the nation turns again to the difficult question of how to discourage welfare dependency, these findings have at least two important implications. First, cutting welfare to teenage parents will probably do little to discourage teen sex, pregnancy, and childbearing. Second, it may have the perverse and unintended consequence of encouraging some of the conditions research shows are associated with teen pregnancy—principally poverty and family dysfunction.

What, then, can we do to discourage long-term welfare dependency? Research suggests a very different set of proposals than those under discussion.

HOW SHOULD WELFARE DEPENDENCY BE DISCOURAGED?

First, start early, to ensure that children enter school with the skills they need to succeed. Second, support parents in the tough job of raising and protecting their children. Third, focus on males as well as females, including men in their 20s, since they are the sexual partners of a large proportion of teenage girls. Fourth, encourage abstinence, but also provide contraceptive information to kids who do have sex. (Research indicates that the most effective sex education programs combine the teaching of abstinence with information on contraception.) Most important, invest time and resources in teens so they will perceive opportunities for themselves and realize the value of staying in school and building a positive future.

Cutting welfare benefits to teen mothers may "end welfare as we know it," but it won't end the underlying problem of teenage pregnancy and childbearing. Meeting that challenge will require a broader and more sustained effort.

PERIODICAL BIBLIOGRAPHY

The following articles have been selected to supplement the diverse views presented in this chapter. Addresses are provided for periodicals not indexed in the *Readers' Guide to Periodical Literature*, the *Alternative Press Index*, the *Social Sciences Index*, or the *Index to Legal Periodicals and Books*.

James Brooke	"Idaho County Finds Way to Chastise Pregnant Teen-Agers: They Go to Court," *New York Times*, October 28, 1996.
William F. Buckley Jr.	"Zounds! Enforcing the Law in Idaho!" *National Review*, August 12, 1996.
Arthur J. Delaney	"The Grotesque World of Today's Sex Education," *New Oxford Review*, May 1996. Available from 1069 Kains Ave., Berkeley, CA 94706.
Elizabeth Gleick	"Putting the Jail in Jailbait," *Time*, January 29, 1996.
Ellen Goodman	"The Revival of 'Shotgun' Marriage," *Liberal Opinion Week*, September 23, 1996. Available from PO Box 880, Vinton, IA 52349-0880.
Debra W. Haffner	"What's Wrong with Abstinence—Only Sexuality Education Programs?" *SIECUS Report*, April 1, 1997. Available from 130 W. 42nd St., Suite 350, New York, NY 10036-7802.
David J. Kalke	"It's Our Duty to Give Away Condoms," *New York Times*, July 8, 1995.
Jane Mauldon and Kristin Luker	"Does Liberalism Cause Sex?" *American Prospect*, Winter 1996.
Ellen Perlman	"The Mother of All Welfare Problems," *Governing*, January 1997.
John Sheffield	"WARNING: Your Theology May Be Fatal to Your Kids," *U.S. Catholic*, July 1996.
Kathleen Sylvester	"Preventable Calamity: How to Reduce Teenage Pregnancy," *USA Today*, March 1997.
Gerald Unks	"Will Schools Risk Teaching About the Risk of AIDS?" *Clearing House*, March 13, 1996. Available from Customer Service, 1319 18th St. NW, Washington, DC 20036.

WHAT ROLE DO THE MEDIA AND GOVERNMENT PLAY IN THE PROBLEM OF TEEN SUBSTANCE ABUSE?

CHAPTER PREFACE

Since the 1980s, drug education programs have become commonplace throughout American schools. The most popular of these programs is DARE (Drug Abuse Resistance Education), which is offered in nearly 75 percent of the nation's school districts. In the DARE program, taught primarily to fifth- and sixth-grade students, a specially trained police officer comes to a classroom once a week for seventeen consecutive weeks. Students are given lessons that include information about the dangers of drug use, role-playing exercises, and group discussions. Variations of the curriculum are taught from kindergarten through high school.

Although DARE is popular, many people question its effectiveness. For example, journalist Jeff Elliott argues that the statistics presented in the lessons are inaccurate. In addition, he contends, the role-playing lessons are not realistic: "When Maggie [a student] role-plays saying no to Officer Campbell, she reinforces her skills at turning down drugs from a uniformed policeman. Not a likely real-life scenario."

The result, these critics assert, is that DARE fails to reduce juvenile drug use. As evidence, they cite reports such as the 1997 *Monitoring the Future Study*, which indicates that drug use among high school seniors has risen since 1994. In that year, 38 percent of high school seniors reported that they had used marijuana or hashish sometime during their life. In 1997, half of all seniors had used marijuana. Being a DARE graduate may even increase the likelihood of drug use, critics maintain. They cite one study that shows DARE graduates are more likely than nongraduates to use marijuana.

Although some studies question DARE's effectiveness, others have indicated positive results. A 1995 evaluation in South Carolina concluded that 77 percent of DARE graduates in one county were not using drugs four years after receiving instruction. Even critics maintain that DARE can succeed. A 1994 study by the Research Triangle Institute (RTI) found that DARE deterred alcohol, tobacco, or drug use in only 3 percent of its participants. However, RTI praised the program's organization and community support and concluded that with some modifications, including more interactive methods, the program can be effective.

Drug education programs are only one factor influencing teen drug use. Other variables include government antidrug efforts and media portrayals of drug use. These and related issues are examined in the following chapter.

| "Material legitimizing drugs can be found in music, film, television, the Internet and mass market outlets."

THE MEDIA ENCOURAGE TEEN SUBSTANCE ABUSE

Barry R. McCaffrey

In the following viewpoint, Barry R. McCaffrey argues that the substance abuse problem among teenagers is due in part to the influence of the media. McCaffrey asserts that sophisticated pro-drug messages are imparted to youths through music, television, the Internet, and other media. He maintains that while free speech must be protected, the media have the obligation to present the dangerous consequences of drug use accurately. McCaffrey is the director of the Office of National Drug Control Policy.

As you read, consider the following questions:

1. How many millions of Americans use drugs regularly, according to the author?
2. In McCaffrey's view, how does the speed of mass communication affect news reporting on the drug abuse issue?
3. According to McCaffrey, what is the biggest challenge faced by those who are combatting the irresponsible portrayal of drugs in the media?

Reprinted from Barry R. McCaffrey, "Mass Manipulation of Young Minds," *Los Angeles Times*, January 2, 1997.

In our national effort to combat substance abuse, the entertainment industry has often been targeted unfairly as the creator of a popular culture that sends inappropriate drug messages to youth. The truth is, Hollywood writers, producers and directors are parents, community leaders and educators—in the best sense of the word—just like the rest of us. Culture is a joint product that the media reflect as much as invent. In fact, most mass media mirror an America envied around the globe. Recent studies show that we do have a problem in terms of rising adolescent drug use, but blame should not be focused on one industry.

One study found that youngsters are less likely to turn to addictive drugs if they have a concerned adult spending time with them. In the wake of shattered families and the need for two-parent wage earners, the adults talking to our children frequently reach them through TV, film, video games, radio, music, the Internet and advertising. We call on the mass media to honor the highest ideals that make the creative arts the repository of our collective cultural heritage.

THE GROWTH IN SUBSTANCE ABUSE

While overall drug use in America has declined for the last 15 years, from 23 million regular users to 12 million, substance abuse among young people has grown since 1992. One-third of eighth-graders report the use of illicit drugs, including inhalants. About 15% admit to having drunk more than five alcoholic beverages in a row during the previous two weeks. The National Survey on Drug Abuse found that marijuana was used by 77% of current drug users (9.8 million of the estimated 12.8 million Americans who used an illicit drug during the month prior to being interviewed). The report, "Cigarettes, Alcohol, Marijuana: Gateways to Illicit Drug Use," showed that children who used marijuana were 85 times more likely to use cocaine. Heroin use among adolescents has doubled. There are 3.6 million Americans hooked on cocaine, heroin, methamphetamines and new "designer" drugs.

In facing the challenge of drug abuse, the media have never been less monolithic. Fragmentation is rampant in the entertainment business. Vertical integration of media conglomerates adds pressure to the marketplace and the creative process. Cable television now cuts into network territory, and competition among stations means that less free air time is available for public service announcements to combat drug use. The number of these has dropped. Commercial forces work against children's programming, where positive role models can be presented, because advertising targets viewers aged 18 to 49 as the prime consumer market.

Changes in viewer habits have also worked against drug education. Channel surfing on a remote control leads TV watchers away from public service announcements.

THE SOPHISTICATION OF PRO-DRUG MEDIA

In general, the speed of mass communication mitigates against exploring an issue carefully as people's attention span decreases in correlation with shorter, rapid-fire presentation. ABC's Ted Koppel has noted that sound bites in news broadcasts have gone down from an average of 22 seconds to eight seconds. Furthermore, pro-drug messages are communicated to our children through the most sophisticated, multimedia techniques while anti-drug forces typically fight back with bumper stickers: that is, with one-dimensional approaches.

The intensification of media effects such as virtual reality has been coupled with a thirst for heightened experience and risk-taking in our culture. Exaggerated proportions and greater degrees of violence are related to this trend. This mentality provides the context for drug use either as a "high" beyond normal experience or as an instant solution to discomfort in a now-oriented society. The glamorization of drugs in "heroin chic" fashions encourages their use. Technology has made America stronger and faster in every respect; the demand for intensity and "speed" through drugs is a negative counterpart to these industrial changes.

THE MEDIA ARE COMPLACENT

The media must share the blame for the fact that so many kids today don't know the perils of drug abuse. When today's teenagers were toddlers, I personally produced two prize-wining television specials about the curse of drug abuse. . . .

These days, no one is clamoring for TV shows or magazine articles about drug abuse. "Been there, done that" is the prevailing attitude.

Carl Rowan, *Liberal Opinion Week*, September 9, 1996.

There have been excellent initiatives such as the push for three hours a week of educational programming, some of which can be devoted to drug education. Mediascope, a non-profit organization that promotes social and health issues, published a nationwide study of media violence. A similar, quantified study of drugs in the media would be useful. In addition there has been considerable interest in media literacy so that children and parents alike will understand how subtle messages influence viewers. ABC, HBO and the Academy of Television Arts and Sciences are developing excellent antidrug campaigns. Programs like ER and NYPD Blue usually depict public health issues accurately, showing the results of destructive behavior. However, the biggest challenge we face today is a willingness by some in the entertainment industry to produce whatever sells.

THE MEDIA'S INFLUENCE

Unfortunately, material legitimizing drugs can be found in music, film, television, the Internet and mass market outlets. Fortunately, consumers are reacting to objectionable messages, and chains like Wal-Mart and Blockbuster Video have decided not to stock CDs and tapes with offensive content.

The influence of the media should not be underestimated. By mid-adolescence, kids have watched about 15,000 hours of television—more time than they spend with teachers in school. Add to that figure the hours devoted to video games, watching tapes on the VCR, listening to the radio and attending movies, and the media's impact becomes primary.

Concerns have arisen periodically in this country over media content. In the continuing dialogue, extremes have been presented on both sides. Free speech as guaranteed in the 1st Amendment to the Constitution must be protected. However, the news and entertainment industries owe it to our youth to portray realistically the dangerous consequences of illegal drug use. Writers and producers of comedy series might think about the impact of "wink and nod" acceptance of illegal drugs as well as blatant pro-drug messages that put teens at risk. A spirit of cooperation is the key to a constructive partnership between the media and the public. The Office of National Drug Control Policy offers support and elicits help in our national challenge to beat back the problem of illegal drugs that threaten America's children.

| "Contrary to the official/media
script, . . . drug abusers are not
getting younger and younger, but
older and older."

THE MEDIA EXAGGERATE THE EXTENT OF TEEN SUBSTANCE ABUSE

Mike Males

The press misstates the true extent of America's drug problem, Mike Males claims in the following viewpoint. Males contends that teenage drug use is not a serious problem; instead, he maintains, the actual drug crisis is among adults. According to Males, adults over age thirty-five represent a significant percentage of overdose deaths and emergency room admittances. In contrast, he maintains, only a small percentage of teenagers use illegal drugs. Males argues that the media are too eager to help politicians blame youths for the nation's drug problem instead of focusing on the dangers of adult drug use. Males is the author of *The Scapegoat Generation: America's War on Adolescents*.

As you read, consider the following questions:

1. According to statistics cited by Males, what percentage of heroin-related emergency room cases in 1995 were due to drug use by patients over age thirty-five?
2. What percentage of youths do not use cocaine or heroin, according to the author?
3. What does Males think is the scariest aspect of the media's failure to acknowledge the adult drug problem?

Reprinted from Mike Males, "Another Anti-teen Fix," *Extra!* November/December 1996, by permission of *Extra!*

With all the obedient indignation of *Pravda* blaring an official diatribe against enemies of the state, the U.S. media has thundered with headlines repeating the official line of an "exploding teenage drug crisis."

THE MEDIA IS ANTI-YOUTH

At least the old Soviet journalists could claim they had no better source of information than state propaganda. What made the American media's anti-youth rampage so reprehensible was that the press did have better information right in reporters' hands. The officials who orchestrated the latest press frenzy actually distributed the excellent 1995 Drug-Related Emergency Department Episodes report by the Drug Abuse Warning Network (DAWN) and the 1995 National Household Survey on Drug Abuse by the U.S. Department of Health and Human Services—confident that few in the press would actually read them.

This official smugness was justified. The press ignored what the reports said and reported only what drug-war interests said the reports said. Shrieking headlines of skyrocketing teen-drug use dutifully ensued, as they do on schedule most every August and December when politicians dispense the latest survey. The media's Teen Armageddon theme was founded in the 1995 Household Survey's finding that 8.2 percent of 12–17-year-olds said they had used marijuana in the previous month, up from 1992's level of 3.4 percent.

Had reporters taken minimal time to examine the data with care (instead of charging out to assess how the hullabaloo affected the Bob Dole–Bill Clinton race), they would have unearthed far more startling and disturbing facts about America's real drug malaise. Contrary to the official/media script, the new reports reconfirmed that drug abusers are not getting younger and younger, but older and older. Said the Household Survey in an ignored finding on "the aging cohort of drug users" whose "severe drug problems" dominate the statistics: "In 1979, 12 percent of patients with cocaine episodes were age 35 and older. By 1985, the percentage was 19, and by 1995 it was 43." For heroin, 55 percent of the emergency room cases in 1995 were over age 35, up from 40 percent just seven years earlier.

The DAWN report revealed that in 1995, the rate of ER treatments for cocaine, heroin and marijuana abuse was about the same for teens and young adults (ages 12–25) as it was in the late '80s—despite all the press nostalgia for Nancy Reagan's "just say no" crusades. But during the last seven years, drug emergencies rose by 150 percent among those over age 35. A whopping 96 percent of the 140,000 hospital ER episodes for cocaine, heroin and marijuana in the first half of 1995 involved adults, and four-fifths involved adults over age 26.

STABLE TEENAGE DRUG USE

Rates of teenagers going to ER for drugs were low and stable in 1995, while those of adults were high and rising—exactly the opposite of what the press reported. The reason for the confusion: Officials cleverly released the new Household Survey at the same time they resurrected DAWN's three-month-old survey of hospital emergency treatments for drug abuse. Their evident hope was that reporters would mix the two surveys up, blame rising teen drug use for rising hospital admissions and ignore the much worse adult problem. The hoax worked like a charm.

Newsweek's eight-page cover-story spread (8/26/96) juxtaposed a chart of drug usage by eighth graders with one showing rising ER visits for heroin. USA Today's (8/20/96) lead sentence read: "Teenage drug abuse has risen sharply since 1992, accompanied by increasing visits to hospitals for drug-related emergencies." Stories in the New York Times (8/21/96) and Los Angeles Times (8/30/96) both linked the rise in drug ER trips to increased teen drug use.

The New York Times story asserted that the "steep decline" in adult drug abuse means fewer modern teens are scared away from drugs by the spectacle of debilitated adult addicts and quoted University of Michigan surveyor Lloyd Johnston: "This generation doesn't know about the dangers of drugs the way the last did." Read the reports! This generation of youths is seeing more drug abuse among its elders—14,000 deaths, half a million ER cases, and 1 million adults undergoing addiction treatment in 1995—than any generation since the late 1960s.

MOST YOUTHS DO NOT USE DRUGS

That may be exactly why the 1995 survey found that nine in 10 youths were not currently illegal drug users, and 99 percent were not users of harder drugs such as cocaine or heroin. The survey documented the low rate of heavy drug use among students as well as long-term studies showing that occasional marijuana use rarely evolves into more serious drug habits (Journal of Abnormal Psychology, 1/88; American Psychologist, 5/90).

The survey demolished the oft-repeated contention that using pot is the "gateway" to harder drugs. The survey reported that 65 million Americans age 12 and older, a legion including 100 percent of the occupants of the Oval Office and House Speakership, had tried marijuana—but only two million were current users of cocaine, crack, heroin or speed. That is, even if every hard-druggie started out smoking marijuana, fewer than 3 percent of marijuana smokers become hard-drug patrons.

Teenage marijuana use, past or present, was hardly a topic to generate headline clarions of doom. So routine is the experience in post-1960 America that Clinton's drug policy chief, Barry McCaffrey, admonished politicians jockeying to exploit drug hysteria to lay off berating their opponents' youthful drug use—the better to unite in berating today's youthful drug use.

Adults Are the Greater Drug Risk

Drug emergency room visits compiled by Drug Abuse Warning Network, 1993

Age	Cocaine	Heroin	Marijuana	Total	Rate*
6–11	7	2	na	9	< 0.1
12–17	1,583	282	4,293	6,158	29.8
18–25	22,077	7,912	9,656	39,645	133.7
26–34	52,715	21,127	9,342	83,184	215.0
35–44	37,477	25,792	4,540	67,809	170.0
45–54	7,669	6,561	959	15,189	55.4
55+	1,789	1,289	376	3,454	6.5
Total	123,317	62,965	29,166	215,448	92.8

*Drug-related ER episodes per 100,000 population in each age group.

Source: Substance Abuse and Mental Health Services Administration, *Preliminary Estimates of Drug-Related Emergency Department Episodes*, December 1994.

Nor, the reports showed, is the problem exclusive to aging "60s druggies." True, Clinton's older Baby Boom cohort, now age 45–54, suffered a skyrocketing death rate from abuse of harder street drugs (such as cocaine and heroin), which is now 13 times higher than found among 1995 high schoolers. But Bob Dole's generation of 55–75-year-olds, who supposedly abstained in their 1940s and 1950s youth, now display death tolls from cocaine and heroin more than double that of today's teens—and escalating rapidly.

If the media wanted to honestly examine the relatively low rate of teenage drug use and even lower rate of drug abuse, they would have focused on medical drugs, not street drugs. The media continue to omit the fascinating fact that in 1995, four times more teenagers received emergency drug treatment after ingesting aspirin or aspirin substitutes (such as Tylenol or Advil) than for all street drugs put together.

No Evidence of Heavy Drug Use

It would be worrisome if solid evidence showed that the young are taking up hard drugs such as barbiturates or heroin, or mixing them with another deadly hard drug, liquor—killer cocktails that sent tens of thousands to early graves in the '60s drug crisis. California, which has the nation's largest drug toll, provides detailed records. In 1970, a shocking 43 percent of California's drug overdose deaths were ages 10–24—nearly all from heroin, pills or dope with booze chasers (*California Vital Statistics*, 1970–94). Proof that when lots of young people abuse hard drugs, lots die.

But there is no indication, either from surveys, ER records, addiction treatment admissions or morgues, that today's young are indulging in the hard stuff in any significant numbers. In 1994, just 5 percent of California's drug overdose dead were under age 25.

But with a servile press, who needs evidence? Recent media have been awash in screams that a heroin craze is ensnaring teens and young adults en masse, including a *USA Today* article (7/19/96) that would embarrass the *National Enquirer*. The piece featured *Sassy* magazine editor Caroline Lettieri's intimation that every 14-year-old in Los Angeles was smoking black-tar smack. (If so, heroin must be safer than Tylenol: L.A. hospitals reported a total of 3,724 heroin emergency treatments in the most recent year, only 14 of which involved teens. But 330 L.A. teens wound up in [the] ER for Tylenol's effects).

USA Today's article brimmed with avowals by so-called "experts" that "heroin is the pot of the '90s" and that "smoking or snorting smack is as commonplace as beer for a younger generation." Right. Reporter Elizabeth Snead failed to cite the Household Survey's finding that only 0.2 percent of youths used heroin in the month before the survey—1/100th of the number who drank beer.

The Real Age of Heroin Users

Newsweek's (8/26/96) cover was graced by a 21-year-old former addict and proclaimed: "Heroin . . . Are Teens at Risk?" The story spent six pages terrorizing parents who "are right to be scared" that hordes of youths are primed by "pop culture images" to follow heroin-plagued celebrities over the cliff—absent evidence that anything of the sort was occurring. In truth, the story admitted in a couple of brief sentences, "kids on dope are still rare" and "most heroin users today are still old-timers."

The drug war's government/corporate fountain of disinformation, the Partnership for a Drug-Free America, launched a new campaign (and unabashed pitch for bucks) painting heroin as a youth scourge (*L.A. Times*, 7/30/96). None of the media hyperventilation mentioned the Household Survey's finding that the only age group to show a significantly "increasing rate of heroin smoking" is "adults age 35 and older." Nor Centers for Disease Control studies showing that much of contemporary heroin abuse is among Vietnam veterans whose postwar traumas were neglected by authorities (*Journal of the American Medical Association*, 2/13/87).

The real story is both the rarity of heroin abuse and the evolution of what was once a young man's drug into a 30-40-50-something peril. In 1995, 55 percent of heroin emergency cases involved persons over age 35. The most dramatic rise by far has been among this older group—up 175 percent since 1990. California, which accounts for nearly half the nation's heroin deaths, exemplifies the astonishing trend. In 1970, 44 percent of its heroin deaths involved victims under age 25; in 1994, just 3 percent did. Not one California teenager died of a heroin overdose in the entire year, as did only 17 adults age 20–24—compared to 485 over age 25.

DESIGNATED SCAPEGOATS

The most striking feature of major media drug stories is their formulaic sameness—indeed, all were scripted by the same few officials and "experts." The media have embraced politicians' tacit ground rule that adolescents are Campaign '96's designated scapegoats, a free-fire zone to be blasted at will. Any politician or interest group may depict youth problems as mushrooming to boost their public images and win funding for their plans to meet the "crisis"; when they want to portray youth problems as declining, the press allows the same interests to grab credit. It's no-lose.

The scariest aspect is that the past half century suggests that epidemics of adult drug abuse forecast similar behaviors among the young. The late-1960s heroin and barbiturate crisis among young adults was preceded by a mushrooming toll of barbiturate addiction, overdose and suicide among grownups of their parents' generation, beginning in the late 1950s and fueled by irresponsible prescriptions issued by physicians. Then as now, officials ignored and denied the adult drug crisis, damaging both parents and their children. As a result, there may be a youth hard-drug crisis on the 1990s horizon as well—one promoted by official dereliction and the media's refusal to expose it, not occasional teen pot smokers.

The media hero of the 1996 drug furor is none other than Bush-era drug czar Bill Bennett, recovering nicotine addict and author of the 1989 National Drug Control Strategy, which ignored the plight of drug addicts and hard-drug abusers and instead demonized casual marijuana smokers (Newsweek, 8/26/96). None of the media mentioned the irony that the Clinton era has fully implemented Bennett's age- and race-tainted policy. During the 1992–94 period, arrests of teens for simple marijuana possession skyrocketed. Federal health and FBI Uniform Crime Reports (1994) show that a black teenager is only one-fifth as likely to die from drug abuse as a white adult, but is 10 times more likely to be arrested for drugs.

No matter. The media chastise Clinton for being soft on druggie kids and trumpet "Back to War" (Newsweek, 8/26/96). The latest round of stories featured reporters angrily denouncing teenagers: "What can you do when children just won't listen?" ABC News scolded in its August 20, 1996, lead story. A better question: What can you do when a free press just won't do its job?

"I'm convinced that the resurgence [in teen drug use] stems in part from the disappearance ... of effective national leadership in the fight against drug use."

AN INADEQUATE GOVERNMENT ANTIDRUG EFFORT HAS CONTRIBUTED TO THE PROBLEM OF TEEN DRUG ABUSE

Rob Portman

In the following viewpoint, Rob Portman argues that the federal government is to blame for the growing problem of teenage drug use. He contends that, instead of reducing the extent of teen drug use, the actions taken by the federal government in the early 1990s worsened the problem. Due to this failure in national leadership, according to Portman, the problem must be dealt with at the community level. He maintains that members of Congress should encourage their constituents to work together on this issue. Portman is a Republican congressman from Ohio.

As you read, consider the following questions:

1. According to the author, what actions taken by President Bill Clinton led to a rise in teenage drug use?
2. Why does Portman want businesses involved in community coalitions?
3. In the author's view, what role can the federal government play in fighting drug abuse?

Abridged from Rob Portman, "Addicted to Failure," Policy Review, September/October 1996, by permission of Policy Review.

In 1995, a 16-year-old constituent of mine, Jeff Gardner, died from a lethal combination of "huffing" gasoline and smoking marijuana. After Jeff's death, his mother, who was aware of a much larger drug problem in the community, called a parent's meeting at the local high school. No one came. She told me her story and asked how her representative in Congress was going to help address the growing drug problem. It was a fair question, but I was not satisfied with the response I could give her.

GOVERNMENT LEADERSHIP IS NEEDED TO REDUCE DRUG USE

Members of Congress take seriously their responsibility to represent their constituents in Washington—by legislating, by voting, and when appropriate, by securing federal funding for state and local concerns. Despite spending $13 billion annually on drug-control programs, however, drug abuse is rising dramatically among our youth (see chart).

A big part of the problem has been President Bill Clinton's failure to show any leadership on this issue (until his wise appointment of General Barry McCaffrey as the new drug czar). In fact, President Clinton hurt the antidrug effort by cutting the Office of National Drug Control Policy from 147 to 25 full-time positions, by hiring a surgeon general who advocated legalization of drugs, by cutting funding for interdiction efforts, and by sending confusing messages about the stigma of illegal drug use. It is no surprise, then, that after dramatic reductions in drug use during the decade before Clinton took office, drug use has nearly doubled among teenagers during his administration. The evidence shows that national leadership is critical in reducing drug abuse.

Jeff's mother wanted that leadership, but in a manner that would help her in Goshen, Ohio. Spending more federal dollars on drug-control programs was unlikely to directly touch this mother's life. Neither would it encourage other parents in her community to address the drug problem. How could I really help? By rolling up my sleeves and providing leadership where it matters most—at the local community level.

Members of Congress are in a unique position to mobilize people in their own communities. By the nature of our jobs, we deal with every sector of the districts we represent. We can also bring statewide and nationwide expertise and resources to bear on a problem. And we can draw the attention of news media that is so critical to educating and mobilizing neighborhoods to solve their toughest social problems. What I've initiated—and what I'm challenging my colleagues in Congress to embrace—is a new model of governance that recognizes the limitations of Washington-based solutions, while drawing on the resources of citizens locally.

CAUSE FOR ALARM

If there is any public-policy area that demands a new, more effective approach, it is drug abuse. Recent Gallup polls show that crime and drugs are Americans' top concerns. When you ask parents and children what is the most serious issue facing youth today, both groups cite drug abuse.

National statistics show there is indeed cause for alarm. After a decade of progress in the war on drugs, the number of young people using drugs began to increase in 1992; use among young kids showed the sharpest increase. LSD use is now at its highest level since 1975, when it was first measured. Since 1992, the number of children between 12 and 17 using marijuana has nearly doubled. To put the problem in perspective, in the average class of 25 eighth-graders (13- and 14-year-olds), five are now using marijuana. And drug abuse is implicated in other social problems—violent crime, dropout rates, and domestic violence, to name a few.

Greater Cincinnati has a drug problem that mirrors the startling national statistics. This region of the country experienced a similar decline in drug use in the 1980s. But by the early 1990s, it began to skyrocket. Why?

I'm convinced that the resurgence stems in part from the disappearance both of effective national leadership in the fight against drug use and of the media attention that usually follows such leadership. This attention is vital to teaching children that drug abuse is both dangerous and wrong.

COMMUNITY ACTIVISM IS CRUCIAL

No one makes this point more authoritatively than Jim Burke, the chairman of the Partnership for a Drug-Free America. It was Burke's group in the 1980s that launched the most extensive and successful public-service campaign in the country. Burke also believes strongly that, while the message must emanate from our national leaders and engage the opinion shapers at every level, this issue is best addressed at the community level.

I decided we could not afford to wait for another tragedy to prompt us to action. Since 1995, I have spearheaded an effort to establish the Coalition for a Drug-Free Greater Cincinnati. This effort is not about flashy press conferences and slick brochures. It's a serious, long-term initiative that brings together for the first time community activists already involved in the antidrug effort, key business figures, religious leaders, the media, parents, young people, law enforcement officials, and others. Our aim is to develop and implement a comprehensive, community-based strategy to reduce drug abuse in our region.

How do you start a coalition? First, you do a lot of listening at all levels—to kids and parents, grass-roots activists, and state and national leaders in the field. Over an 18-month period, we led or helped organize countless meetings in all sorts of settings, from living rooms to classrooms, and from boardrooms to community centers. . . .

LOSING THE WAR AGAINST ADDICTION

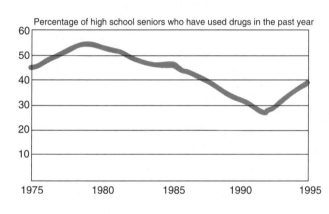

Percentage of high school seniors who have used drugs in the past year

Source: Monitoring the Future Study, University of Michigan, December 1995.

Work is a good place to find parents who need counsel on dealing with teenage drug use. So we had to engage businesses. . . .

We also brought the National Parents' Resource Institute for Drug Education (PRIDE), a premier national parents' group, to one of our school districts to train more than 600 parents in taking practical steps to keep their kids drug free. . . .

The list of initiatives proposed by the local community, brought to the coalition by state and national leaders, and facilitated by congressional leadership, goes on and on. . . .

FINDING A NEW APPROACH

The public rightly expects the federal government to do something about drug abuse, which diminishes and threatens the lives of so many of our young people. And the federal government clearly has an important role in combating drug abuse:

protecting our borders and interdicting drugs from other countries, strengthening our federal criminal-justice system, and providing federal assistance for the best prevention and treatment programs.

Despite a significant federal effort, however, our country is still seeing dramatic increases in drug use among our teenagers. In the last two years alone, use of illegal drugs has increased 50 percent. We need a new approach.

Many of my colleagues are beginning to agree. At least 15 other members of Congress are establishing, or supporting, similar community coalition efforts in their regions. The entire House of Representatives—in an unusual show of election-year bipartisanship—recently endorsed this community-based initiative.

That's a much more significant step than cynics imagine. Although the public has become disenchanted with the federal government's ability to address our worst social problems, there's still an abiding faith in a community's ability to fashion solutions close to the needs of ordinary people. And members of Congress can still be a catalyst. Although the public seems to distrust Congress as a whole, individual members are generally well respected in their districts.

The point is that members of Congress *can* and *should* inspire citizens to action. We've heard about the need to revitalize civil society. Well, here's a concrete example of how members of Congress can do that in a way that actually touches people's lives—not by passing more laws in Washington, but by using their bully pulpits to engage their communities back home. This is how we as national leaders can best exert—and sustain—national leadership over the long haul.

And for the sake of the Jeff Gardners in our communities, we'd better get started.

> "You wonder just how much impact
> federal drug policy has on a
> teenager's propensity to smoke a
> joint."

An Inadequate Government Antidrug Effort Is Not Responsible for Teen Drug Abuse

Jacob Sullum

Many conservative politicians have blamed the rise of teenage drug use on the government's lack of effort in fighting the problem. In the following viewpoint, Jacob Sullum contends that this argument is unconvincing because government antidrug efforts have intensified, as evidenced by the fact that arrests for drug offenses are increasing. Sullum argues that the real reason teenage substance use has risen is that government antidrug efforts—including drug education programs and antidrug advertising campaigns—are ineffective in altering the behavior of teenagers. Sullum is a senior editor at *Reason*, a monthly libertarian magazine.

As you read, consider the following questions:

1. What cultural indicators does the author believe reflect the increase in teenage drug use?
2. According to Sullum, how many drug arrests were there in 1994?
3. How do adolescents define "cool," according to the author?

Reprinted, with permission, from Jacob Sullum, "Drug Charge," *Reason*, March 1996. Copyright 1996 by the Reason Foundation, 3415 S. Sepulveda Blvd., Suite 400, Los Angeles, CA 90034; www.reason.org.

Teenage drug use is up and Orrin Hatch says it's Bill Clinton's fault. "President Clinton has been AWOL—absent without leadership—on the drug issue," the chairman of the Senate Judiciary Committee said at a December 1995 press conference. "Ineffectual leadership and failed federal policies have combined with ambiguous cultural messages to generate changing attitudes among our young people and sharp increases in youthful drug use."

It's tempting to dismiss Hatch's remarks as partisan posturing. But history teaches us to be on guard when politicians start warning that the nation's youth are in peril. After all, parental alarm helped set off the wave of anti-drug hysteria that swept the nation in the 1980s.

THE TEENAGE DRUG CULTURE

And Hatch is right about one thing: Drug use by teenagers seems to be rising. In the 1992 National Household Survey on Drug Abuse, 4 percent of respondents in the 12-to-17 age group reported using marijuana during the previous month. That figure rose to 4.9 percent in 1993 and 6 percent in 1994. The increase in marijuana use was the main reason for the rise in past-month illegal drug use, which went from 6.1 percent in 1992 to 8.2 percent in 1994. Those figures follow a 13-year decline, and they are still less than half the peak levels seen in 1979. But the rise seems to be more than a blip. The trend can also be observed in cultural indicators such as the movie *Dazed and Confused*, caps embroidered with cannabis leaves, the popularity of the pot-obsessed rap group Cypress Hill, and the *Saturday Night Live*–inspired catch phrase, "you can put your weed in there."

Hatch's explanation for the trend—Clinton's lack of enthusiasm for the war on drugs—is unconvincing. For one thing, Clinton, like his Republican predecessors, has requested ever-escalating anti-drug budgets. Hatch says more of that money should be spent on interdiction. But a wide range of drug policy specialists, including congressional researchers and scholars at the RAND Corporation, have concluded that beefing up interdiction is not a cost-effective way to raise retail prices or reduce availability.

HARSHER GOVERNMENT POLICIES

Hatch also charges Clinton with neglecting enforcement. Yet during his administration the number of Americans in state and federal prisons surpassed 1 million for the first time, largely because of harsh sentences for drug offenses, and the United States now has the highest incarceration rate in the world. The total number of drug arrests reached a record 1 million in 1994, about 43 percent more than in 1991. Nearly half of those arrests were for marijuana, most for simple possession. Says Allen St. Pierre, deputy national director of the National Organization for the Reform of Marijuana Laws, "These data confirm that the federal government's war on marijuana consumers has gotten significantly tougher under Clinton's regime."

DRUG EXPERIMENTATION DOES NOT CAUSE ADDICTION

The vast majority of kids who experiment with dope will not become drug addicts. . . .

Contrary to anti-drug propaganda, you can experiment with illicit drugs and still go on to live a successful and productive life. Contemplating the latest report [on the rise in adolescent drug use], we ought to keep in mind the reassuring certainty that most of the teen-age users won't still be using drugs a decade from now.

Stephen Chapman, *Conservative Chronicle*, September 4, 1996.

Which makes you wonder just how much impact federal drug policy has on a teenager's propensity to smoke a joint. Another puzzle: The same surveys that find an increase in teenagers' use of marijuana and LSD also find an increase in their use of tobacco and alcohol. In the Household Survey, for example, the percentage of 12-to-17-year-olds who reported smoking cigarettes during the previous month rose from 9.6 in 1992 to 18.9 in 1994. Past-month alcohol use rose from 15.7 percent in 1992 to 21.6 percent in 1994. In proportional terms, marijuana use increased more than alcohol use but less than cigarette use. Enforcement of the laws forbidding sales of tobacco and alcohol to minors has never been very effective, but there's no reason to believe it has been especially lax in recent years.

FAILED PROPAGANDA

On the other hand, during the last decade both legal and illegal drugs have been the targets of pervasive propaganda, much of it government-sponsored, aimed at convincing kids to stay away from them. Posters and TV ads depict smokers as disgusting, inconsiderate, and antisocial. Drug Abuse Resistance Education (DARE) communicates an all-or-nothing, "Just Say No" message to elementary-school students. A typical fifth-grader exposed to DARE at a Los Angeles school where my wife taught wrote an essay in which she pledged never to drink beer or smoke pot, because she wanted to attend college, get married, and raise a family—accomplishments that exposure to alcohol or marijuana would make impossible. Commercials from the Partnership for a Drug-Free America portray pot smokers as lazy, stupid, and unattractive. Their vivid images (the fried egg/brain, the diver jumping into an empty pool) warn of disastrous consequences from experimenting with illegal drugs.

Those scare tactics may work over the short term, but they tend to backfire as kids get older. For one thing, teenagers discover through personal observation that much of what they've been told about drugs is nonsense. (Drug warriors are alarmed that the percentage of high school seniors who think smoking marijuana poses a "great risk" has dropped, but the truth is that smoking marijuana *doesn't* pose a great risk.) Perhaps more important, many adolescents define *cool* as whatever most offends adults. Which may explain why tobacco's popularity has increased the most.

| "Saving our children from a lifetime
addiction is going to take all of us.
. . . from business to government at
the Federal, State and local levels; to
young people themselves."

THE GOVERNMENT SHOULD COMBAT TEEN SMOKING

Donna E. Shalala

Donna E. Shalala is the secretary of the U.S. Department of Health and Human Services. In the following viewpoint, she argues that teenage smoking is a growing and critical problem that needs to be tackled with government actions and community assistance. Shalala advocates restrictions on advertising so that parents, not tobacco companies, will be the ones to educate children about smoking. This viewpoint is taken from a speech given by Shalala on May 29, 1996, at the National Tobacco Control Conference in Chicago. Some of the proposals mentioned in the viewpoint, such as restrictions on tobacco advertising, were later included in a settlement reached between the tobacco industry and the attorneys general of forty states. As of this writing, the terms of the settlement had not been approved by Congress. However, R.J. Reynolds Tobacco Company agreed to stop using Joe Camel in its advertisements by September 1998.

As you read, consider the following questions:

1. At what age does the average smoker start smoking, according to Shalala?
2. What is the goal of the Clinton administration's proposals, according to the author?
3. What does Shalala believe the entertainment industry can do to reduce teenage smoking?

Reprinted from Donna E. Shalala, "Smoking and Youth," a speech delivered at the National Tobacco Control Conference, May 29, 1996, Chicago, Illinois.

F ifty years ago, an ad appeared in *Life Magazine* proclaiming, "More doctors smoke Camels than any other cigarette."

That was then. This is now: Television and radio airwaves no longer carry commercial jingles touting the "pleasures" of smoking and smokeless tobacco. And parents and children are now armed with powerful information in the battle to save their health and maybe even their lives.

THE TOBACCO WAR IS UNFINISHED

Yes, we have "come a long way, baby." But our journey is not over.

Not when more than 90 percent of 6-year-olds can identify Joe Camel as a symbol of smoking.

Not when 77 percent of high school students who tried were able to buy cigarettes in stores—without showing proof of age.

Not when smoking among high school students has climbed about 25 percent since 1992.

Not when the smoking rates for African American males in high school have almost doubled since 1992.

Not when 45 percent of white male high school students use smokeless tobacco or cigarettes.

And not when the average smoker starts at age 14½ and becomes a daily smoker before age 18.

Smoking is a pediatric disease—that must be stopped.

YOUNG PEOPLE SPEAK OUT

Just listen to what our young people have to say:

This from a 16-year-old girl: "I'd like to be a model. Smoking burns off a lot of calories."

A teenager says: "My nerves are bad. Smoking calms me down."

One girl started smoking at 14 because, "All these really cool girls were doing it. I thought they looked so cool."

Every time a child lights up a cigarette, the future of our country hangs in the balance.

Every time a child lights up a cigarette, who knows what brilliant minds and bright dreams will fade into the bleak backdrop of disease and premature death? Future world-class athletes, future computer giants, future educators, and maybe even future Presidents.

Every young person we can save today is another smoke-free adult tomorrow.

The tobacco culture has essentially functioned as a "third parent" for American children: Enticing them with attractive images, playing upon their desire to be glamorous, luring them with T-Shirts and trinkets, and giving them easy ways to obtain cigarettes from vending machines and even free giveaways.

GOVERNMENT TAKES A STAND

There is not a parent in America who wants their children to endure the suffocating death grip of emphysema or lung cancer.

That's why we're working with you to implement the Synar regulations [legislation named after Congressman Mike Synar that requires states to enforce their bans on tobacco sales to minors or lose federal anti-drug abuse funding]—and help states flash a red light on the sale of cigarettes to minors.

That's why we are helping support local community-based groups through the National Cancer Institute and the Centers for Disease Control and Prevention.

And that's why we're continuing to support research that sheds light on why children start smoking—and what we can do to help stop them.

But now, we have an opportunity to stand with parents and do even more.

We have an opportunity to strike a big blow—a winning blow—against underage smoking in this country.

Never before in history. Let me repeat: Never before in history has a President had the courage and conviction to take on the fight against tobacco—in the name of public health and the name of our children. I am proud of that—and I know you are too.

THE PRESIDENT'S PROPOSAL

Overall, our goal is to reduce smoking among children and adolescents by 50 percent within seven years. And, to do that, President Bill Clinton has offered some of the boldest public health proposals this country has ever seen:

To reduce the access and appeal of tobacco to children, we propose to limit all the easy ways that children get tobacco, keep tobacco billboards at least 1,000 feet from our children's schools, take the Marlboro Man and Joe Camel out of publications read by millions of children, and prohibit tobacco companies from using the allure of their name brands in sponsoring events.

Some might say: "Can't parents take care of their children?" The answer is, "Of course they can."

That's precisely the point of our proposal: To make sure that parents—not the tobacco culture—are in control when it comes to educating children about an addiction that could take years off their lives.

Our proposal is about putting power back into the hands of parents—where it belongs. And, it's all part of our comprehensive strategy to help parents steer their precious children away from all the dangerous minefields like drugs, tobacco, pregnancy, AIDS and violence—and towards healthy, productive futures.

Are these important steps? Absolutely.

Source: Rob Rogers. Reprinted with permission from United Feature Syndicate.

With the Food and Drug Administration proposed rule, we would reduce kids' access to tobacco and the substantial appeal created by $6 billion of advertising and promotion.

The President has put forth a comprehensive and effective proposal to reduce children's use of cigarettes and smokeless tobacco.

The President's mark is the right one.

I know some of you may be wondering about the possibility of finding a legislative solution to this problem.

In August 1995, in the East Room, the President said he would rather put these restrictions into law immediately through legislation than wait for a long regulatory proceeding.

An Inadequate Response

The President has reiterated this point, by saying: "If the tobacco companies will voluntarily accept legislation containing limits that will be as effective as what we propose, I will say, again, we believe it's better to have the companies come forward and ask for legislation."

Let me be clear: When we are shown a bill that is as effective and meaningful as the measures the President has proposed, we will enthusiastically work with Congress.

But Philip Morris and United States Tobacco's proposal falls short of that mark. For example, under their proposal, the Marlboro Man would still ride the billboard prairies and rope our children in.

Our children would still be able to walk into stores and grab a pack of cigarettes from a self-service display. And Joe Camel would still pop up in magazines read by lots of children—offering concert tickets in exchange for a lifetime of addiction.

That is not good enough.

If the companies seriously engage Congress, and Congress gets to work on legislation that meets the President's mark, he is ready. Meanwhile, we will continue to work on the President's initiative.

Support is Vital

We will not—let me repeat—we will not retreat from our commitment to the health of our children. And, I know you won't either.

But government cannot do it alone—and we shouldn't ever try.

It's going to take leaders who speak to children every day—from the family rooms to the classrooms, and from the televisions to the soccer fields.

We need to reach children where they live, where they learn, and where they hang out—with words and images they understand.

That's why we're teaming up with leaders throughout the media and entertainment industries—from daytime talk show hosts to TV producers to the editors of popular magazines.

Some people say that we're wasting our time trying to work with the entertainment industry. They say that the industry will never change and that the proper role for government is merely to shake a finger at them. But, I strongly disagree.

I don't have the luxury or the desire to give up on people who speak to millions of children each day.

You're looking at a huge movie fan—and I know that this industry is savvy and talented enough to create characters who are cool enough not to smoke.

That's the challenge I brought to industry leaders when I visited California in April 1996—to use their enormous power the right way. And, that's the message we need to send to role models all over America: "Our children are watching your example." The question is, what lessons will they learn?

From the PTA, parents are learning how they can act today to help their children avoid tobacco and addiction tomorrow.

From Major League Baseball and Oral Health America, they're learning about the tragic effects of smokeless tobacco.

From the American Medical Association, the American Cancer Society, the American Lung Association, the American Heart Association, the American Academy of Pediatrics, and others, communities are learning how to protect children from tobacco—school by school, block by block, home by home.

And, from the U.S. National Women's Soccer team, they're learning that like oil and water, tobacco and fitness just don't mix.

FIGHTING SMOKING AT THE COMMUNITY LEVEL

Saving our children from a lifetime addiction is going to take all of us. From parents to teachers; from coaches to clergy; from business to government at the Federal, State and local levels; to young people themselves.

Because, the battle against underage smoking will only be won at the community level by leaders like you—leaders who forge strong partnerships. And leaders who marry vision with action to stop smoking before it even starts.

I want you to know that our Administration remains 100 percent committed to the effective work you do at the State, local and community levels. And we must continue to support your community-based initiatives now and into the future.

With your leadership, we have an opportunity to return power to parents and communities.

We have an opportunity to change the course of deadly diseases.

We have an opportunity to help children avoid the shadow of nicotine addiction—protecting our best and smartest investment for the future.

And, if we win this battle, we have an opportunity to fundamentally change the course of history—and do something that historians will no doubt record as the most important public health triumph of our time.

It can be done. It must be done. And, working together, it will be done.

"*We all agree underage teenagers shouldn't smoke; that's not the issue. The issue is whether the FDA should launch yet another extravagant regulatory crusade.*"

GOVERNMENT EFFORTS TO COMBAT TEEN SMOKING ARE UNNECESSARY AND WASTEFUL

Part I: Edwin Feulner; Part II: D. T. Armentano

In Part I of the following two-part viewpoint, Edwin Feulner argues that the tobacco regulations proposed by the Food and Drug Administration (FDA) in an attempt to reduce teenage smoking are counterproductive. He contends that the regulations could actually entice teenagers to smoke by making smoking seem rebellious. In Part II, D. T. Armentano maintains that restrictions on tobacco advertising are unnecessary because teen smoking is a less extensive problem than the FDA claims. Feulner is the president of the Heritage Foundation, a conservative Washington-based think tank. Armentano is professor emeritus of economics at the University of Hartford in Connecticut. Some of the FDA's proposals cited in the viewpoint became part of a settlement reached in June 1997 between the tobacco industry and the attorneys general of forty states; however, as of this writing, Congress had not approved the settlement.

As you read, consider the following questions:

1. According to Feulner, who is better qualified than the FDA to address the issue of teenage smoking?
2. In Armentano's view, what would be the actual impact of the tobacco regulations?

Part I: Reprinted from Edwin Feulner, "FDA: The Smoking Police," at http://seldy.townhall.com/heritage/commentary/of-ef14.html, cited March 4, 1998, by permission of the author. Part II: Reprinted from D.T. Armentano, "Teen Smoking: The New Prohibition," *The Freeman*, January 1997, by permission of *The Freeman*.

I

Is the government supposed to protect us from everything that could possibly harm us? Or are there some areas where we should be responsible for taking care of ourselves?

RESTRICTIONS ON TEEN SMOKING

Take teenagers and smoking. The Food and Drug Administration (FDA) and its Commissioner David Kessler are getting ready to pounce on America with a litany of new regulations aimed at stopping teens from smoking.

The FDA's proposed restrictions include:

- Banning cigarette vending machines and self-service displays in stores;
- Requiring tobacco companies to launch a $150 million-per-year nationwide TV ad campaign to discourage underage smoking;
- Banning the use of tobacco brand names on T-shirts, hats, keychains and lighters; and
- Banning brand-name sponsorship of sporting events, such as the Virginia Slims tennis tournament.

Of course, we all agree underage teenagers shouldn't smoke; that's not the issue. The issue is whether the FDA should launch yet another extravagant regulatory crusade whose nuisance value will likely outweigh any benefits.

UNNECESSARY RAIDS

Remember: this is the FDA that conducted the 1991 raid that captured 24,000 half-gallons of Citrus Hill "fresh choice" orange juice, all because the agency didn't like the way the o.j. was labeled! Are the food and drug police now going to swoop down on every mom and pop grocery store to make sure teen employees aren't smoking in the boy's room?

Apparently so. Since 1990, the FDA's staff has grown from 7,600 to 8,700, and its budget has ballooned from $598 million to $760 million. They've got to do something with all that extra manpower and money.

So, now they're going to send out an army of regulators whose job will be to make sure mom and pop conceal cigarettes from view—as if this ever stopped a teenager from doing something he or she was determined to do. Store workers will have to take time out to deal with every tobacco transaction, since cigarettes will only be sold from behind the counter and not from self-service displays. The watchdogs will probably even send in teenagers paid to test the system. If something slips through the cracks, out come the handcuffs!

REGULATIONS LEAD TO REBELLION

Come on. American University student and former Heritage Foundation intern Jennifer Murray may have said it best in an essay when she accused President Bill Clinton of forgetting what it's like to be a teenager. "Formula-One racing cars painted with tobacco company logos, billboards at sports events, advertisements in magazines (particularly of those men on horseback)— none of these had anything to do with my [former] tendency to light up," Jennifer confessed. "The main contributor was something President Clinton's 'solutions' would only encourage: rebellion." The new federal regulations, far from preventing teens from smoking, "by focusing additional attention on the forbidden, could actually entice them," Jennifer warns.

Isn't there someone more qualified than the FDA orange juice police to address this issue? Such as parents?

Let's get real. As Jennifer pointed out, "Banning cigarette ads and vending machines will do more for President Clinton's wavering image than it will for teens." Does anyone really believe the president is lying awake at night worrying about teen smoking? I kinda doubt it. But he is worried about being popular.

Smoking sure isn't as popular as it used to be. And everybody cares about kids.

You do the math.

II

The expressed goal of the Clinton Administration's proposed regulations on cigarettes and smokeless tobacco products is to reduce adolescent consumption by one half. Roughly three million American juveniles smoke and an additional one million young males use smokeless tobacco. Putting aside (for the moment) all of the other difficulties with the new regulations, can they possibly accomplish their objective?

NO DIRECT RELATIONSHIP

The government proposes severe new restrictions on the advertising of cigarettes under the mistaken assumption that there is a direct relationship between advertising and the decision to begin smoking. But there is little reliable evidence in the literature to support this contention and plenty of evidence to contradict it.

Juvenile smoking actually increased in Finland after a complete ban on tobacco advertising was implemented in 1978.

Norway, which completely prohibited tobacco advertising in 1975, has a higher percentage of juvenile smokers than does the United States. And black teens in the United States, presumably exposed to the same "persuasive" advertising as white teens, have far lower smoking rates.

Do Not Discriminate Against Smokers

Smokers have become disenfranchised and dehumanized; they are non-people. To talk about them would pollute the moral purity of the anti-smoking crusade. Smoking is unhealthy; lowering it among teens would be good. But how much is society entitled to punish adult smokers to protect teens? How much should society discriminate against a large class of people (smokers) whose behavior offends—but does not threaten or impoverish—the larger public? And how much can society change teens, who consistently defy what their elders think best?

Robert J. Samuelson, *Washington Post*, February 25, 1998.

It is widely acknowledged (outside of Washington) that the decision to start using tobacco products is influenced primarily by culture, family, and peer pressure, not corporate advertising. So banning brand-name event sponsorships, or limiting cigarette brand logos on race cars and drivers' uniforms, will have no measurable effect on any ten-year-old's decision to light up.

Teenage Smoking Has Decreased
Food and Drug Administration (FDA) Commissioner David Kessler would have us believe that billboards near playgrounds and the use of cigarette brand names on t-shirts (which would all be prohibited under the new regulations) have created a teen-smoking health epidemic. Nonsense. The marginal increase in teen smoking recorded since 1991 is easily swamped by the longer-term steadily *downward* trend.

Listening to the FDA one would never know that the percentage of high school seniors who smoke daily has fallen from over 28 percent in 1977 to less than 20 percent in 1994. Heavy smoking (half a pack or more per day) among high school seniors had declined from 17.9 percent in 1975 to approximately 11 percent today. Yet the Administration now proposes to restrict tobacco advertising in teen oriented magazines to a black-and-white, text-only format even though there is no evidence that such publishing censorship would impact teen cigarette consumption.

The bottom line is that these new regulations have little to do with changing cigarette consumption by teenagers. What they will do, however, is hurt certain advertisers, promoters of sporting events, tobacco manufacturers and their employees, and vending machine owners. Even more importantly, they will enhance the power of government bureaucrats to exercise additional control over private markets and lifestyles. And that's what the antismoking crusade is really all about.

TOBACCO REGULATIONS ALREADY EXIST

Make no mistake about it. The FDA would like to severely restrict the sale of *all* cigarettes in the United States. The Administration knows that total prohibition is politically impractical at the moment so it starts the crusade with regulations that aim to "protect the children." And when these fail, as they must, the regulators will return with stronger recommendations and sterner controls.

But controls are already a way of life in this industry. Laws addressing tobacco sales to minors are on the books in every state and the District of Columbia. Dozens of governmental agencies, including the Department of Health and Human Services, the Federal Trade Commission, and the Bureau of Alcohol, Tobacco and Firearms, already police and regulate the industry. Every state taxes cigarettes and most lump a sales tax on top of the excise tax. Cigarettes are already among the most taxed and regulated products in America.

The Administration has invited public comment, so it should be told that its new regulations will not affect teen smoking but will, instead, reduce employment and income in tobacco-related industries. It should also be told that its contrived rationale to regulate cigarettes as a "medical device" is as phony as a three-dollar bill. Finally, it should be told that freedom and persuasion, not censorship or regulation, are the primary social values that we choose to pass on to our children . . . whether they smoke or not.

PERIODICAL BIBLIOGRAPHY

The following articles have been selected to supplement the diverse views presented in this chapter. Addresses are provided for periodicals not indexed in the *Readers' Guide to Periodical Literature*, the *Alternative Press Index*, the *Social Sciences Index*, or the *Index to Legal Periodicals and Books*.

James Bovard	"Unsafe at Any Speed," *American Spectator*, April 1996.
Stephen Chapman	"Washington Cannot Solve the Drug Problem," *Conservative Chronicle*, September 4, 1996. Available from PO Box 37077, Boone, IA 50037-0077.
Sarah Glazer	"Preventing Teen Drug Use," *CQ Researcher*, July 28, 1995. Available from 1414 22nd St. NW, Washington, DC 20037.
Daniel R. Levine	"Drugs Are Back—Big Time," *Reader's Digest*, February 1996.
Mike Males	"High on Lies: The Phony 'Teen Drug Crisis' Hides the Deadly Truths of the 'War on Drugs,'" *Extra!*, September/October 1995.
Barry R. McCaffrey	"Prevention Programs Work," *Vital Speeches of the Day*, November 15, 1996.
Lance Morrow	"Kids and Pot," *Time*, December 9, 1996.
New York Times	"The Attack on Teen-Age Smoking," August 11, 1995.
Rob Portman and Bob Dole	"Preventing Teen Drug Abuse," *Christian Science Monitor*, February 27, 1996.
Carl Rowan	"Who's to Blame for Drug Use, Smoking?" *Liberal Opinion Week*, September 9, 1996. Available from PO Box 880, Vinton, IA 52349-0880.
Jacob Sullum	"Weed Whackers," *Reason*, November 1996.
Wall Street Journal	"Drugs and God," March 6, 1996.
Christopher S. Wren	"Marijuana Use by Youths Rebounding After Decline," *New York Times*, February 20, 1996.
Mortimer B. Zuckerman	"Great Idea for Ruining Kids," *U.S. News & World Report*, February 24, 1997.

FOR FURTHER DISCUSSION

CHAPTER 1

1. Of the factors discussed in this chapter, which do you think contributes most to teen problems? Explain your answer. What factors not mentioned by the authors might put teens at risk?

2. Mona Charen argues that media violence encourages teens to engage in violent behavior. Mike Males maintains that real violence, not media violence, is to blame. Whose argument do you find more convincing, and why?

3. Edward Grimsley contends that adults' inconsistent messages about morality confuse teenagers. What examples of mixed messages does he provide? Do you agree with Grimsley's assertion that adults are hypocritical about issues of morality? Why or why not?

CHAPTER 2

1. Roger L. Conner is the executive director of an organization that seeks to balance individual liberties and community responsibility. George Brooks is a jail chaplain in Chicago. How do you think their affiliations influence their views on the rights of gang members? Explain.

2. Margaret Beyer bases her argument that juvenile boot camps are a failure partly on evidence that such programs do not reduce recidivism. Eric Peterson acknowledges that boot camps do not decrease recidivism, but he cites statistics showing that boot camps can improve participants' educational skills and increase employment. Can these camps be considered successful if they do not reduce the number of repeat offenders? Why or why not? If increased academic achievement and employment for these teenagers is desired, which programs do you think are more effective—boot camps or the programs described in Beyer's viewpoint? Explain your reasoning.

3. The authors in this chapter offer a variety of solutions to the problem of teenage crime and violence. Which solution(s) do you believe is most effective? What other approaches do you think might work? Explain your answers.

CHAPTER 3

1. The authors of the viewpoints in this chapter discuss four different methods for preventing teenage pregnancy. Which methods do you feel would help reduce teenage pregnancy?

Which would be ineffective? Support your answers with references to the viewpoints.

2. Maggie Gallagher maintains that parents can successfully encourage teenagers to abstain from sex. M. Jocelyn Elders, on the other hand, contends that most teens have sex and therefore need to be educated about preventing pregnancy and sexually transmitted diseases. Which argument do you find more convincing, and why? Is it inevitable that teenagers will have sex? Why or why not?

3. Ralph deToledano argues that the enforcement of statutory rape laws can reduce teen pregnancy. Catherine Elton disagrees. How do these authors view relationships between adult males and teenage girls? How do their differing views about these relationships influence their opinions about enforcing statutory rape laws?

CHAPTER 4

1. Barry R. McCaffrey contends that the media popularize and legitimize drug use. He asserts that the media should present the destructive results of substance abuse. Do you find his argument convincing? Why or why not?

2. Rob Portman argues that teen drug use should be combated on a community level, claiming that the federal effort has been inadequate. Jacob Sullum contends that the federal government has intensified its antidrug efforts but that those efforts fail because they place too great an emphasis on inaccurate propaganda. Should teenage substance abuse be fought on a federal or local level? What are the advantages and disadvantages of both approaches? Explain your answers.

ORGANIZATIONS TO CONTACT

The editors have compiled the following list of organizations concerned with the issues debated in this book. The descriptions are derived from materials provided by the organizations. All have publications or information available for interested readers. The list was compiled on the date of publication of the present volume; the information provided here may change. Be aware that many organizations take several weeks or longer to respond to inquiries, so allow as much time as possible.

Advocates for Youth
1025 Vermont Ave. NW, Suite 200, Washington, DC 20005
(202) 347-5700 • fax: (202) 347-2263
info@advocatesforyouth.org
web address: http://www.advocatesforyouth.org
Advocates for Youth believes young people should have access to information and services that help prevent teen pregnancy and the spread of sexually transmitted diseases and enable youth to make healthy decisions about sexuality. The organization publishes brochures, fact sheets, and bibliographies on adolescent pregnancy, adolescent sexuality, and sexuality education.

The Alan Guttmacher Institute
120 Wall St., New York, NY 10005
(212) 248-1111 • fax: (212) 248-1951
e-mail: info@agi-usa.org • web address: http://www.agi-usa.org
The institute works to protect and expand the reproductive choices of all women and men. It strives to ensure people's access to the information and services they need to exercise their rights and responsibilities concerning sexual activity, reproduction, and family planning. Among the institute's publications are the books *Teenage Pregnancy in Industrialized Countries* and *Today's Adolescents, Tomorrow's Parents: A Portrait of the Americas* and the report "Sex and America's Teenagers."

American Civil Liberties Union (ACLU)
132 W. 43rd St., New York, NY 10036
(212) 944-9800 • fax: (212) 869-9065
e-mail: aclu@aclu.org • web address: http://www.aclu.org
The ACLU is a national organization that works to defend Americans' civil rights as guaranteed by the U.S. Constitution. It opposes curfew laws for juveniles and others and seeks to protect the public-assembly rights of gang members or people associated with gangs. The ACLU's numerous publications include the briefing papers "Reproductive Freedom: The Rights of Minors," "Point of View: School Uniforms," and "Equality in Education."

**The National Center on Addiction and
Substance Abuse at Columbia University (CASA)**
152 W. 57th St., 12th Fl., New York, NY 10019-3310
(212) 841-5200 • fax: (212) 956-8020
web address: http://www.casa.columbia.org

CASA works to combat all forms of substance abuse and to study the
links between substance abuse and other societal problems, including
crime, homelessness, and teen pregnancy. The center publishes reports
and surveys on the cost, impact, and prevention of substance abuse, including "Substance Abuse and the American Adolescent," "Rethinking
Rites of Passage: Substance Abuse on America's Campuses," and the
CASA 1997 Back to School Survey, all of which are available on-line.

National Council on Alcoholism and Drug Dependence (NCADD)
12 W. 21st St., New York, NY 10010
(800) 622-2255 • (212) 206-6770 • fax: (212) 645-1690
e-mail: national@ncadd.org • web address: http://www.ncadd.org

In addition to helping individuals overcome addictions, NCADD advises the federal government on drug and alcohol policies and develops substance abuse prevention and education programs for youth. It
publishes fact sheets and pamphlets on substance abuse, including the
titles *Youth and Alcohol* and *Who's Got the Power? You . . . or Drugs?*

National Institute of Justice (NIJ)
810 Seventh St. NW, Washington, DC 20531
(202) 307-2942
e-mail: askncjrs@ncjrs.org
web address: http://www.ojp.usdoj.gov/nij/

NIJ is the primary federal sponsor of research on crime and its control.
It sponsors research efforts through grants and contracts that are carried out by universities, private institutions, and state and local agencies. Its publications include the research briefs *Gang Crime and Law Enforcement Recordkeeping* and *Street Gang Crime in Chicago.*

National Institute on Drug Abuse (NIDA)
U.S. Department of Health and Human Services
5600 Fishers Ln., Rockville, MD 20857
(301) 443-6245
e-mail: information@lists.nida.nih.gov
web address: http://www.nida.nih.gov

NIDA supports and conducts research on drug abuse—including the
yearly Monitoring the Future Survey—in order to improve addiction
prevention, treatment, and policy efforts. It publishes the bimonthly
NIDA Notes newsletter, the periodic *NIDA Capsules* fact sheets, and a cata-
log of research reports and public education materials, such as "Marijuana: Facts for Teens."

National School Safety Center (NSSC)
4165 Thousand Oaks Blvd., Suite 290, Westlake Village, CA 91362
(805) 373-9977 • fax: (805) 373-9277
e-mail: june@nssc1.org • web address: http://www.nssc1.org

NSSC is a research organization that studies school crime and violence, including hate crimes. The center believes that teacher training is an effective means of reducing these problems. Its publications include the book *Gangs in Schools: Breaking Up Is Hard to Do* and the *School Safety Update* newsletter, which is published nine times a year.

Office for Victims of Crime Resource Center
810 Seventh St. NW, Washington, DC 20531
(800) 627-9872
web address: http://www.ojp.usdoj.gov/ovc

Established in 1983 by the U.S. Department of Justice's Office for Victims of Crime, the resource center is a primary source of information regarding victim-related issues. It answers questions by using national and regional statistics, research findings, and a network of victim advocates and organizations. The center distributes all Office of Justice Programs publications, including *Female Victims of Violent Crime* and *Sexual Assault: An Overview*.

Office of Juvenile Justice and Delinquency Prevention (OJJDP)
633 Indiana Ave. NW, Washington, DC 20531
(202) 307-5911 • fax: (202) 307-2093
e-mail: askjj@ojp.usdoj.gov
web address: http://www.ncjrs.org/ojjhome.htm

As the primary federal agency charged with monitoring and improving the juvenile justice system, the OJJDP develops and funds programs on juvenile justice. Among its goals are the prevention and control of illegal drug use and serious crime by juveniles. Through its Juvenile Justice Clearinghouse, the OJJDP distributes fact sheets and reports such as "How Juveniles Get to Criminal Court," "Gang Suppression and Intervention: Community Models," and "Minorities and the Juvenile Justice System."

Partnership for a Drug-Free America
405 Lexington Ave., 16th Fl., New York, NY 10174
(212) 922-1560
web address: http://www.drugfreeamerica.org

The Partnership for a Drug-Free America is a private, nonprofit coalition of professionals from the communications industry. Based on the belief that changing attitudes is the key to changing behavior, the partnership's mission is to reduce demand for illegal drugs by changing public attitudes about drugs through the media. The partnership's website includes an on-line database of drug information, news about media efforts to stop drug abuse, and other resources for parents and teens.

Suicide Awareness\Voices of Education (SA\VE)
PO Box 24507, Minneapolis, MN 55424-0507
(612) 946-7998
e-mail: save@winternet.com • web address: http://www.save.org

SA\VE works to prevent suicide and to help those grieving after the suicide of a loved one. Its members believe that brain diseases such as depression should be detected and treated promptly because they can result in suicide. In addition to pamphlets and the book *Suicide: Survivors—A Guide for Those Left Behind*, the organization publishes the quarterly newsletter *Afterwords*.

Suicide Information and Education Centre
#201 1615 Tenth Ave. SW, Calgary, AB T3C OJ7, CANADA
(403) 245-3900 • fax: (403) 245-0299
e-mail: siec@nucleus.com • web address: http://www.siec.ca

The Suicide Information and Education Centre acquires and distributes information on suicide prevention. It maintains a computerized database, a free mailing list, and a document delivery service. It publishes the quarterly *Current Awareness Bulletin* and the monthly *SIEC Clipping Service*.

BIBLIOGRAPHY OF BOOKS

Alan Guttmacher Institute — *Sex and America's Teenagers*. New York: Alan Guttmacher Institute, 1994.

S. Beth Atkin — *Voices from the Streets: Young Former Gang Members Tell Their Stories*. Boston: Little, Brown, 1996.

William J. Bennett, John J. DiIulio Jr., and John P. Walters — *Body Count: Moral Poverty ... and How to Win America's War Against Crime and Drugs*. New York: Simon & Schuster, 1996.

Bureau of Justice Assistance — *Addressing Community Gang Problems: A Model for Problem Solving*. Washington, DC: Bureau of Justice Assistance, January 1997. Available from http://www.ojp.usdoj.gov/BJA.

Phyllida Burlingame — *Sex, Lies, and Politics: Abstinence-Only Curricula in California Public Schools*. Oakland, CA: Applied Research Center, 1997.

Michael Carrera — *Adolescent Sexuality and Pregnancy Prevention: Replication Manual*. New York: Bernice and Milton Stern National Training Center for Adolescent Sexuality and Family Life Education, 1996.

Glenn Alan Cheney — *Drugs, Teens, and Recovery: Real-Life Stories of Trying to Stay Clean*. Hillside, NJ: Enslow, 1993.

Janet Ollila Colberg — *Red Light, Green Light: Preventing Teen Pregnancy*. Helena, MT: Summer Kitchen Press, 1997.

Robert Coles et al. — *The Youngest Parents: Teenage Pregnancy as It Shapes Lives*. Durham, NC: Center for Documentary Studies, 1997.

James E. Cote and Anton L. Allahar — *Generation on Hold: Coming of Age in the Late Twentieth Century*. New York: New York University Press, 1996.

Herbert C. Covey, Scott Menard, and Robert J. Franzese — *Juvenile Gangs*. Springfield, IL: Charles C. Thomas, 1997.

David H. Demo and Anne-Marie Ambert, eds. — *Parents and Adolescents in Changing Families*. Minneapolis: National Council on Family Relations, 1995.

Shirley Dicks, ed. — *Young Blood: Juvenile Justice and the Death Penalty*. Amherst, NY: Prometheus Books, 1995.

Linnea A. Due — *Joining the Tribe: Growing Up Gay and Lesbian in the '90s*. New York: Anchor Books, 1995.

Irving B. Harris — *Children in Jeopardy: Can We Break the Cycle of Poverty?* New Haven, CT: Yale University Press, 1996.

James C. Howell	*Juvenile Justice and Youth Violence.* Thousand Oaks, CA: Sage, 1997.
Yusuf Jah and Sister Shah'Keyah	*Uprising: Crips and Bloods Tell the Story of America's Youth in the Crossfire.* New York: Scribner, 1995.
Janice Joseph	*Black Youths, Delinquency, and Juvenile Justice.* Westport, CT: Praeger, 1995.
Malcolm W. Klein	*The American Street Gang: Its Nature, Prevalence, and Control.* New York: Oxford University Press, 1995.
Kristin Luker	*Dubious Conceptions: The Politics of Teenage Pregnancy.* Cambridge, MA: Harvard University Press, 1996.
Barbara S. Lynch and Richard J. Bonnie, eds.	*Growing Up Tobacco Free.* Washington, DC: National Academy Press, 1994.
Mike Males	*The Scapegoat Generation: America's War on Adolescents.* Monroe, ME: Common Courage Press, 1996.
Joseph Marshall Jr. and Lonnie Wheeler	*Street Soldier: One Man's Struggle to Save a Generation—One Life at a Time.* New York: Bantam Doubleday Dell, 1996.
Karin A. Martin	*Puberty, Sexuality, and the Self: Boys and Girls at Adolescence.* New York: Routledge, 1996.
Rebecca A. Maynard, ed.	*Kids Having Kids: Economic Costs and Social Consequences of Teen Pregnancy.* Washington, DC: Urban Institute Press, 1997.
James B. McCarthy	*Adolescence and Character Disturbance.* Lanham, MD: University Press of America, 1995.
Barbara A. Miller	*Teenage Pregnancy and Poverty: The Economic Realities.* New York: Rosen, 1997.
Jeffrey L. Morelock	*Drugs in High School: The Disturbing Truth.* St. Petersburg, FL: Guideline, 1995.
National Institute on Drug Abuse	*Drug Abuse Prevention for At-Risk Groups.* Washington, DC: U.S. Department of Health and Human Services, 1997.
Office of Juvenile Justice and Delinquency Prevention	*Urban Delinquency and Substance Abuse.* Washington, DC: U.S. Department of Justice, March 1994.
Gary Remafedi, ed.	*Death by Denial: Studies of Suicide in Gay and Lesbian Teenagers.* Boston: Alyson, 1994.
Elizabeth A. Ryan	*Straight Talk About Drugs and Alcohol.* New York: Facts On File, 1995.
William B. Sanders	*Gangbangs and Drive-Bys: Grounded Culture and Juvenile Gang Violence.* New York: Walter de Gruyter, 1994.

Gini Sikes

8 Ball Chicks: A Year in the Violent World of Girl Gangsters. New York: Doubleday, 1997.

Judie Smith

Drugs and Suicide. New York: Rosen, 1995.

Irving A. Spergel

The Youth Gang Problem: A Community Approach. New York: Oxford University Press, 1995.

Lee G. Streetman

Drugs, Delinquency, and Pregnancy: A Panel Study of Adolescent Problem Behaviors. New York: Vantage, 1996.

Sharon Thompson

Going All the Way: Teenage Girls' Tales of Sex, Romance, and Pregnancy. New York: Hill and Wang, 1995.

Margi Trapani

Reality Check: Teenage Fathers Speak Out. New York: Rosen, 1997.

U.S. Senate Subcommittee on Juvenile Justice

Juvenile Crime: Breaking the Cycle of Violence: Hearing Before the U.S. Senate Committee on the Judiciary, November 29, 1994. Washington, DC: U.S. Government Printing Office, 1996.

INDEX

Drug Education (PRIDE), 157
National Review, 118, 120
Netherlands, 113, 116
Neuhaus, Richard John, 120
New Jersey, 30, 68, 97
New Republic, 129
Newsweek, 25, 47, 149, 151, 153
New York, 68, 132
New York City, 30, 31, 59, 97
New York Times, 149
Norplant, 115, 118, 121, 124
   promiscuity encouraged by, 122-23
Norway, 171
NYPD Blue, 146

Office of Justice Programs (OJP), 89
   Boot Camp Technical Assistance
      Workshop, 91
Office of Juvenlie Justice and
   Delinquency Prevention (OJJDP), 85,
   86, 87, 89, 92
Office of National Drug Control Policy,
   146, 155
Ohio, 92, 155, 156
   see also Cleveland
Oregon, 57
Outside In (counseling agency), 57,
   58, 60

Paducah, Kentucky, school shooting, 65
Pantelides, Edith A., 123
Parachini, Allan, 83
Parent, Dale, 91-92
Parker, Tyrone, 103
Partnership for a Drug-Free America,
   152, 162
Peele, Stanton, 26
Pennsylvania, 68, 94
   see also Philadelphia
Person, Terry, 57, 58, 60
Peterson, Eric, 85, 175
Philadelphia, Pennsylvania, 66, 102,
   167
Planned Parenthood, 109
Policy Review, 110
Popenoe, David, 16
Portman, Rob, 154, 176
Poynter, Chris, 88
Psychological Bulletin, 4 F

Quayle, Dan, 16, 34

racism, 82, 123-24, 153
RAND Corporation, 160
Rector, Robert, 126
rehabilitation programs
   community, 84
   successful, 94

see also boot camps
Reiss, Ira, 112
Reno, Janet, 101
Reproductive Health Matters, 123
Republican Party, 79
Resolving Conflict Creatively Program
   (RCCP), 97
Rights of Lesbians and Gay Men
   committee, 59
risk factors faced by teenagers
   exaggeration about, 25
      due to adult bias against teens, 26
      preventive measures undermined
         by, 28
   increased by inconsistent morality, 52
      and mixed messages from adults,
         40, 53-55
   interrelatedness of, 19, 124
   lack of adult care, 36-37
   variety of, 17-22
   ways to combat, 22-23
   see also child abuse; media; single-
      parent families
Rowan, Carl, 145

Samuelson, Robert J., 172
Sandefur, Gary, 50
San Francisco, California, 57, 58
Sassy magazine, 151
Schmidt, Fran, 98
school dropout, 20, 21
school violence. *See* Jonesboro,
   Arkansas, school shooting; youth
   violence
Schwartz, Amitai, 77
sex education, 139
   European, 113-14
   inadequacy of, 112
   and loss of moral standards, 54, 55,
      127
   and role of parents, 109-10
   should focus on abstinence, 108-10
   should focus on contraceptives and
      protection, 111-14
Sexuality Information and Education
   Council of the United States
   (SIECUS), 112
sexually transmitted diseases, 43, 113,
   114, 124
   see also AIDS
Shalala, Donna E., 134, 103
Shapiro, Joseph P., 127
Shriver, Timothy, 98
single-parent families, 20
   biased media reports about, 45-46
   children of, can be successful, 47, 49
   increasing numbers of, 18, 38, 135
   many variables among, 50

188